A Complete Guide to Fishing

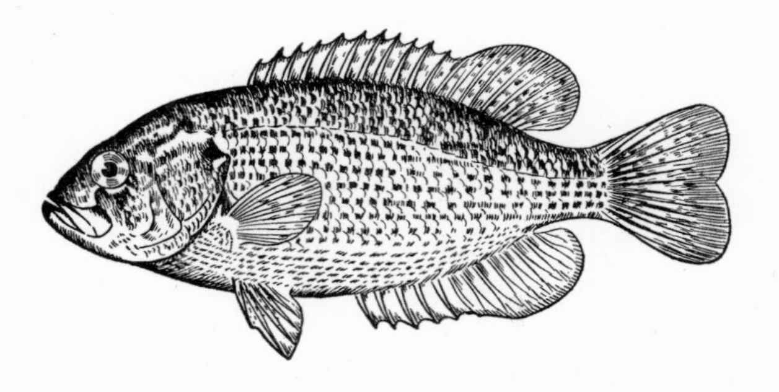

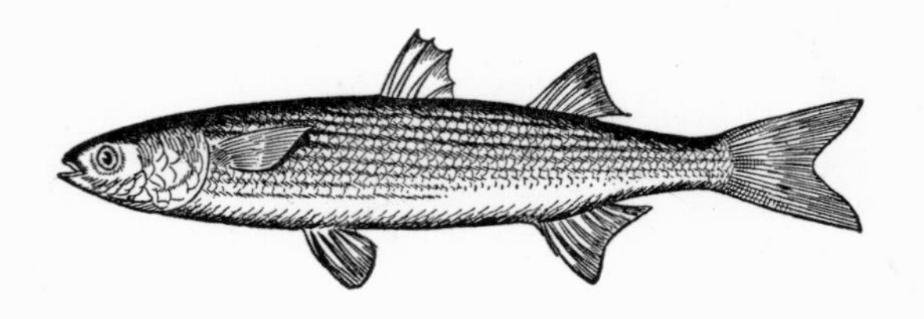

A Complete Guide to Fishing

BY VLAD EVANOFF

Illustrated by the Author

THOMAS Y. CROWELL COMPANY
NEW YORK

Manufactured in the United States of America by the Vail-Ballou Press, Inc., Binghamton, New York
Library of Congress Catalog Card No. 61-7618
Second Printing

Introduction

Men have been fishing on this earth since earliest times. The first fishermen caught fish with their bare hands, and later with spears, nets, crude hooks, and lines. But they caught fish for food. It is only in the last few hundred years that fishing has become a sport. Fish are still caught for food; but millions of people all over the world are now fishing just for fun. Fishing is easily the most popular participant sport in this country, with more than 25 million devotees.

It is exciting to see a big fish swimming in the water, then watch as he comes up and takes your bait or lure. The strike, the leap of a hooked fish, the run in which line is taken off the reel at great speed, the battle to land a large fish you have hooked—all these experiences are tremendously stirring when your fish is powerful or cunning.

If you catch a record fish you may want to have it mounted, and you may win a prize in one of the many fishing contests run each year. You will surely take a photograph of a good catch or of the big one you got, and it will be a proud moment when you show the photo to your family and friends.

Fishing is a healthy pastime. It keeps you out in the open for hours, breathing fresh air and getting beneficial exercise. When you wade a trout stream or walk along the surf for some distance, when you row a boat, and, of course, when you cast repeatedly, you are constantly bringing many muscles into play.

On the other hand, if you are tired or feel lazy, you can sit on the shore or in a boat and relax all day long. You can set your own pace.

Many of the fish you catch will be good to eat. After a day of fishing there is nothing more delicious than fresh fish fried to a crisp, golden brown—especially when you caught them yourself.

Another advantage of fishing is that you can do it by yourself. Naturally, you will often go fishing with friends or with your family. But you don't need a team of a certain number of people to go fishing. You can go alone or with a friend and have just as much fun as being with a large group.

One of the best things about fishing is that you don't need a lot of money to take part in the sport. Of course, some kinds of fishing require expensive tackle and the chartering of a large boat. But there are many kinds which do not require much money. You can fish a near-by lake or stream with an inexpensive or even homemade rod, and with bait dug out of your own back yard.

Fishing can be practiced over a long season. You can start early in the spring and continue well into the fall. You can even go ice fishing and codfishing in the winter if you live in the right surroundings. And of course, if you live in Florida or near other tropical waters, you can fish all year round.

Not only can you fish all through the year, you can fish all through your life. Young people like to play baseball, basketball, or football, but as they grow older they lose both interest and ability. This almost never happens with fishing. Once you become a fisherman you remain a fisherman; it is truly a lifetime sport.

Although luck plays a part in fishing, there is also a great deal of skill and knowledge involved. In the long run, the man who catches the most fish is the one who knows what fishing tackle to use, which lure or baits are best and how to present them, where to find the fish and how to go after them. But nobody ever becomes perfect at fishing: there is always something new to learn.

Contents

CONTENTS

CONTENTS

A Complete Guide to Fishing

1 · Still-Fishing Tackle

If you want to fish in a near-by fresh-water lake or stream, but have no fishing tackle, you don't have to wait until you can get a rod and reel. You can have a lot of fun doing still-fishing at a cost of a few pennies. Still-fishing means fishing from shore, a dock, or an anchored boat. You use a live or natural bait, such as a worm or minnow, and drop it into the water, where it remains in one place. Millions of people go still-fishing, and it's a good way to catch many kinds of fresh-water fish.

You can start with an ordinary drop line or hand line. This is about 50 feet of heavy cotton, linen, or nylon line wound on a stick or wood frame for convenient carrying. Tie a sinker to the end of the line.

Then tie one or two hooks on short nylon leaders and tie the leaders just above the sinker. Bait the hooks with live worms or minnows. Then unwind the line from the holder and coil it in a circle on the ground. Tie the hand end of the line to a stake, bush, or tree. Now pick up the coiled line, twirl it around and around, and let the sinker and baited hooks fly out into the water. Let the sinker and baited hooks lie still on the bottom. When you get a bite, tug the line quickly in order to set the hook and then pull in the fish.

Drop lines are best for big fish such as carp and catfish. For more sport with the smaller fish, a pole is often used. If you live in the country, find a good, straight sapling for a fishing pole. You can make the sapling lighter by removing the bark. A sapling cut from a birch or alder tree is best, but any young, straight, thin tree that you can find in the fields or woods will do.

If you live in a city or town, you can buy a bamboo or cane pole in almost any fishing tackle or hardware store. A pole about 10 or 12 feet long is the best length. Cane poles come in one piece or in two or three sections. A one-piece cane pole is excellent if you live near the water where you will fish. But if you must travel to reach the fishing area, a cane pole which comes in sections is easier to carry on a bicycle or in a car, bus, or train.

You can also buy fiber-glass poles for still-fishing, but these are somewhat more expensive. These glass poles are made of hollow tubes which slide in and out like a telescope. They measure 4 or 5 feet when closed, and open to 10 feet or more for fishing. Such hollow glass poles are very strong and light and will last a long time.

In addition to the pole, you need fishing line. You can use any strong line, but braided or twisted nylon or Dacron fishing line testing 18, 20, or 25 pounds is the most suitable. The line should be almost as long as the pole. Tie one end of the line to the pole. Then get nylon leader material, which comes in coils and can be bought in any fishing tackle store. About 12- or 20-pound test nylon is best. Cut off 3 feet of this nylon leader and tie it to the end of the line. To

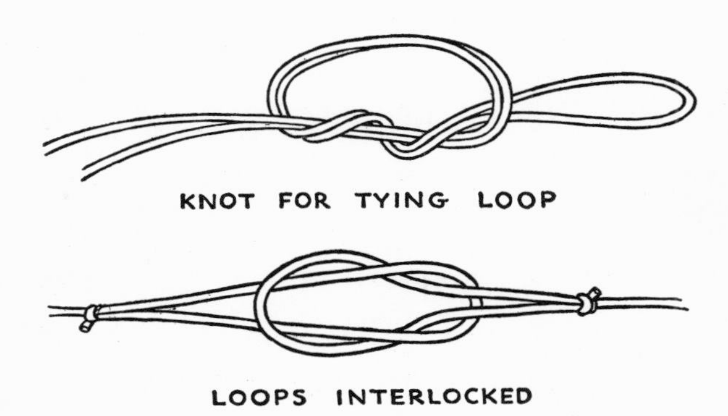

do this make two loops; one tied in the end of the line, the other in the nylon leader. Then interlock them as shown in the drawing.

Next make a float or bobber, using a cork bottle stopper and a wooden matchstick or any small, thin stick. Make a hole through the center of the cork from one end to the other with a nail or an ice pick. Then push the end of the leader through this hole with a stick. Slide the cork up the line about 3 or 4 feet, and push the matchstick through the hole to keep the cork from sliding down the line. (See the drawing.) You can also buy a float or bobber, made from wood, cork, plastic, or porcupine quills, in any fishing tackle store.

To complete the still-fishing outfit you need hooks. The parts of a hook are called the shank, the

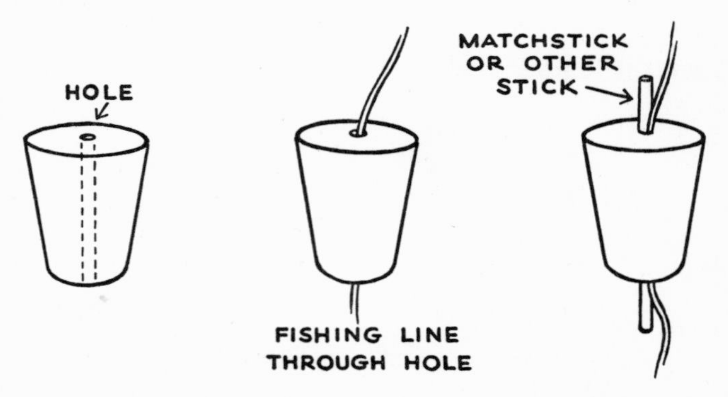

MAKING BOBBER OR FLOAT FROM CORK BOTTLE STOPPER

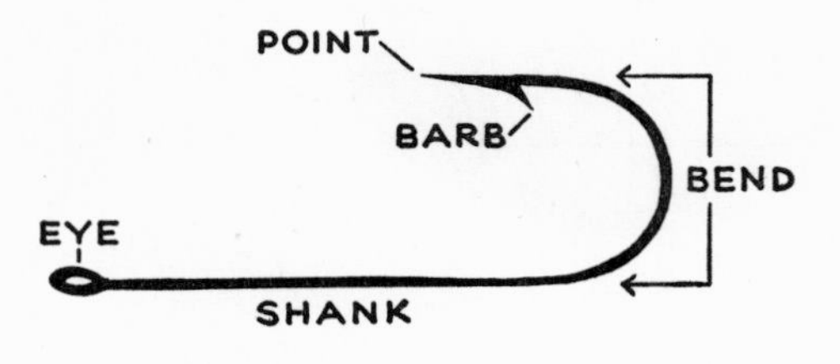

PARTS OF A HOOK

bend, the eye, the barb, and the point, and are shown in the illustration above. Hooks come in different sizes, shapes, and bends, depending on the fish to be caught. For small fish, for example, a hook with thin wire is strong enough. But for big fish you need a heavier wire, which is often flattened or forged to give it still more strength. For fresh-water fishing the most popular patterns of hooks are the Sproat, the Aberdeen, the Carlisle, the Round Bend, and the Wide Bend. Another very good hook is the Eagle Claw, which can be used for most fresh-water fish. It has a rolled-in point shaped like an eagle's talon or claw. This helps to hook and hold a fish securely.

The size of the hook you use will depend on the fish you expect to catch. As a general rule, the small fish with small mouths require smaller-size hooks than the bigger fish with big mouths. The best sizes to buy are Nos. 8, 6, 4, 2, and 1 for such small fish as sunfish, yellow perch, suckers, crappies, and trout. For bass, pickerel, carp, and catfish sizes 1/0, 2/0, and

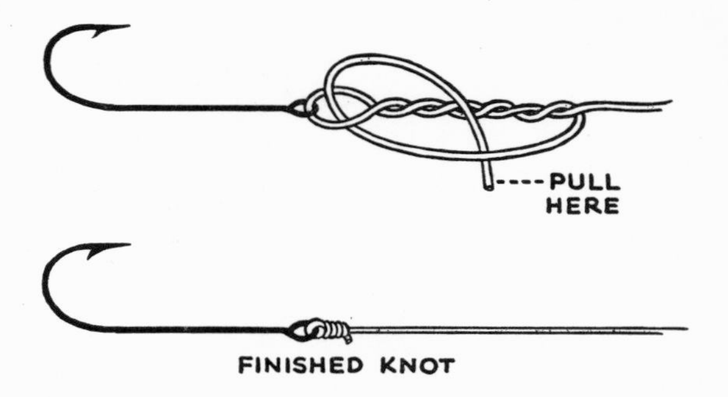

IMPROVED CLINCH KNOT

3/0 or larger are often required. You can buy hooks loose by the dozen, or in boxes of 100 of one size, or you can get a whole box of assorted hooks in different sizes for about 50 cents.

Tie the hook directly to the leader. A good knot to use for tying a hook to a leader is the improved clinch knot, shown in the illustration.

The most important thing to remember about hooks is that the points should always be sharp. Feel the point with your thumb, and if it feels dull, sharpen it with a small file or a sharpening stone. If a hook is rusted, throw it away. Rusty hooks are weak and may break when you hook a big fish.

Usually there is no need for a sinker when you do still-fishing. But if the current is strong, or the bait rises to the top, or if you have to cast out a hand line some distance, use a Split-shot or Clincher sinker on

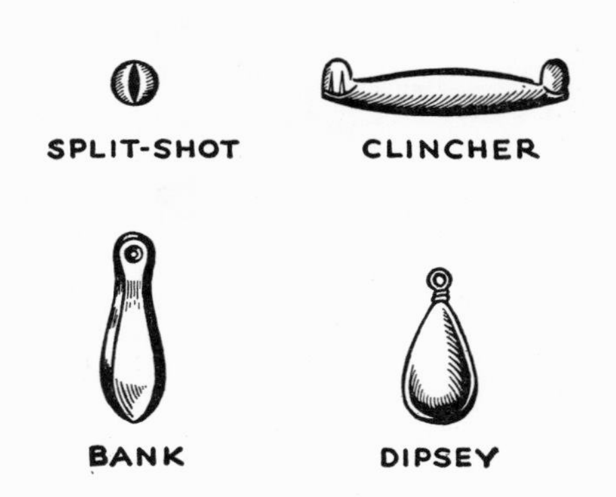

TYPES OF FRESH-WATER SINKERS

your leader. If you fish for catfish or carp you may have to use a Dipsey or Bank sinker to keep the bait lying on the bottom of the river or lake. The different kinds of sinkers are shown in the drawing.

For still-fishing you will also need live bait, such as worms, minnows, frogs, crayfish, grasshoppers, or other insects.

You don't need a big tackle box to hold your still-fishing tackle. An old tobacco can or other small wood or metal box will hold all your hooks, leaders, and sinkers so that they can be carried in your pocket; or else you can buy a small transparent plastic box with many compartments of different sizes to hold your tackle. If you fish from a boat or stay in one spot all day, you can use a large tackle box. These boxes can be bought in any sporting goods store, or you can make one yourself.

2 · Spinning Tackle

Rods · Reels · Lines · Accessories · How to spin cast

Since its introduction from Europe, spinning has become the most popular method of fresh-water fishing in this country. This is partly because spinning tackle makes casting easy. Spin casting is less tiring than either bait casting or fly casting, and there are no backlashes such as those found in bait casting. The rods, reels, and lines are much lighter, and you can cast all day without getting tired. And you can cast from any position or spot: sitting down, standing up, with steep banks behind you, or trees overhead.

Spinning tackle also catches more fish both for the beginner and for the expert angler. The thin, almost invisible lines used in spinning easily fool fish.

In addition, you use smaller, lighter lures with spinning tackle than with bait-casting tackle, and these fool fish that would avoid the larger, heavier lures. Therefore, if you can afford only one fresh-water fishing outfit, you will do well with a spinning rod and reel.

Rods

Most spinning rods are made of glass, hollow or solid. Solid glass spinning rods are cheaper and are very strong. But they are a bit heavier and haven't as good action as a hollow glass rod. The hollow rod is therefore preferable.

For general fishing a medium spinning rod is a good buy. This rod will be 6½ or 7 feet long and can cast lures weighing from ¼ to ⅝ ounce. You can use this rod for fishing in lakes, streams, and rivers for most fresh-water fish.

If you plan to fish mostly for trout in small streams or for small fish such as pan fish in small ponds, a light spinning rod is better. This rod will be 6 or 6½ feet long and can cast lures weighing from 1/16 to ½ ounce.

If you will fish in big lakes or wide rivers for large fish such as pike, muskellunge, carp, catfish, salmon, or steelhead, you should get a heavy spinning

CLOSED TYPE OF SPINNING REEL

rod, from 7 to 8 feet long and casting lures weighing from ½ to 1 ounce.

Spinning rods come in one or two pieces. A one-piece rod is a bit stronger and has better action but is difficult to carry. A two-piece spinning rod is handier and preferred by most fishermen.

Reels

The reel is the most important part of spinning equipment. You can save money by buying a cheaper spinning rod, but get the best reel you can afford. It will give you less trouble and last much longer and be less expensive in the end.

There are two main types of spinning reels, the open reel and the closed reel. The closed spinning reel has a cone-shaped housing over the end of the spool which hides the line from view. The line comes out of a small hole at the pointed end of this cone.

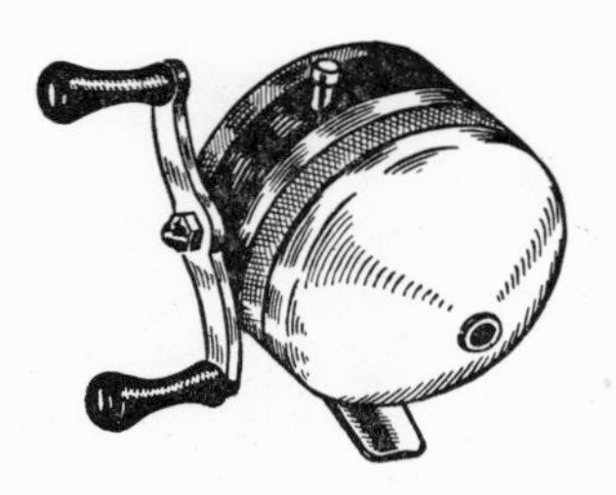

SPIN-CASTING REEL

You press buttons or levers to release the line when casting. This spinning reel is very simple to use and is the most popular with beginners.

There is a second kind of closed reel, called a spin-casting reel. This reel, instead of hanging under the rod as do the two regular spinning reels, is attached above the rod. And regular spinning reels have the handles for winding in the line on the left side; the spin-casting reel has them on the right.

The open spinning reel has an exposed spool so that the line is visible. There is a "bail" pickup which catches the line and guides it to a roller which winds it back on the reel spool after a cast.

Any one of these three reels will enable you to cast far and to catch fish. The closed spinning reel or the spin-casting are best for most fishermen. They work simply and give less trouble than the open spinning reel. The advantages of the open reel are that it has a larger spool than a closed reel and holds

OPEN TYPE OF SPINNING REEL

more line; an open reel is best for use with very light spinning lines; and you can change spools more easily, so that if you have two or three reel spools with different strength lines you are prepared to fish for all kinds of fresh-water fish.

If you plan to fish only a few times a year, get a closed reel or a spin-casting reel. But if you plan to fish often and in different waters and for different kinds of fish, an open spinning reel will be more useful.

Lines

The closed reel or spin-casting reel come with line wound on the spool. Open reels come empty, but some fishing tackle stores will fill the reel with line at a slight extra charge. The lines used with spinning reels and rods are made from braided nylon, Dacron, or monofilament nylon. Most fishermen use the monofilament line, called "mono." It is almost invisible, wears long, and casts smoothly.

Spinning lines usually come on 100-, 200-, or 300-yard spools. Most fresh-water spinning reels hold up to 200 or 300 yards of line; find out how much your reel holds before buying line.

The size and strength of the line are important. The thinner the line, the farther you can cast. If you have a light spinning rod and fish mostly for trout or pan fish, you can use a line testing 3 or 4 pounds. With a medium spinning rod you can use lines testing 6 pounds. For the heavier spinning rods and when fishing in waters filled with weeds, lily pads, logs, or rocks, a line testing 8 or 10 pounds is best.

It is a good idea to buy one or two extra spools for your spinning reels, filled with different strength lines. In this way you can change to a lighter or heavier line to suit the fishing conditions.

To the line you should attach 6 or 7 feet of nylon monofilament leader material, testing 2 or 3 pounds more than the line, using the interlocking loop knots described in the previous chapter. For quick changing of lures, a snap-swivel at the end of the leader is a good idea.

Although you can buy the spinning reel, rod,

and line separately, you can often save money and get a more balanced spinning outfit by buying it in a complete kit. This includes the spinning reel, rod, line, and perhaps a few lures, packed in a big box. If you get a spinning kit, one in the medium-price range is generally a good buy.

Accessories

When you go spin fishing certain accessories will make your fishing trip more comfortable and successful. If you fish a trout stream you'll need a pair of rubber hip boots in shallow water, or a pair of waders reaching your waist or armpits in deeper rivers.

Because you cannot lift a fish into a boat or onto shore with the thin lines used in spin fishing, you will need a landing net. There are many kinds of landing nets, small ones for trout and larger ones for big fish.

You also need a fairly large tackle box to hold the different lures. Such boxes come in various sizes and shapes and are made from steel, aluminum, fiber glass, plastic, or wood. The aluminum, fiber glass, and plastic tackle boxes are most popular because they are strong and light. Tackle boxes usually have swinging or cantilever trays with many compartments for holding the fishing lures.

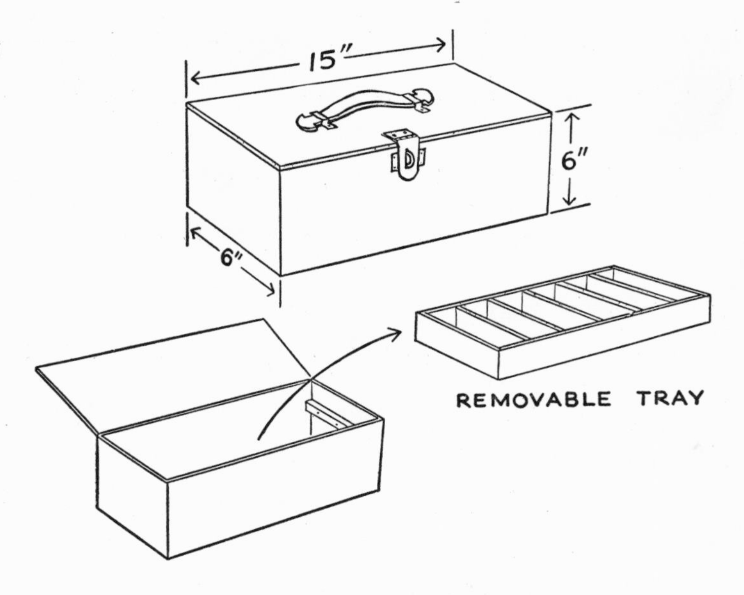

HOMEMADE TACKLE BOX

You can also make your own tackle box from wood. You can buy the wood in almost any lumber-yard. The boards should be ⅜ or ½ inch thick. Plywood, which is lighter and thinner than regular wood, is a good material. A good size for the tackle box is 15 inches long, 6 inches wide, and 6 inches high. There should be a tray inside which can be lifted out and is divided into compartments to hold the fishing lures. Two strips of wood, one at each end of the box on the inside, will keep the tray from falling to the bottom. You also need two hinges, a handle, and a hasp or lock to keep the tackle box closed. After you have finished making the box you should give it at least two coats of either paint or varnish.

The hooks and sinkers used for spin casting are the same as those described in Chapter 1.

How to spin cast

Before casting with a spin reel and rod make sure the spool is properly filled with line, neither too full nor too spare. If it is too full, the line will jump off the spool; if it is too spare you won't be able to cast any distance.

You can practice casting from the shore of a lake or river. If you have no water near by, you can cast over a lawn or field. For practice casting you should buy a small rubber casting weight in any fishing tackle store, or make a casting weight yourself from a round piece of wood and a screw eye. Simply screw the eye into the wood and tie your line to it. A newspaper or a large piece of cardboard makes a good target.

To cast, hold the rod with the right hand above the reel which hangs under the handle. The thumb rests on top of the rod handle while two fingers are in front of the reel support or leg. The other two fingers are behind this support. (See illustration.)

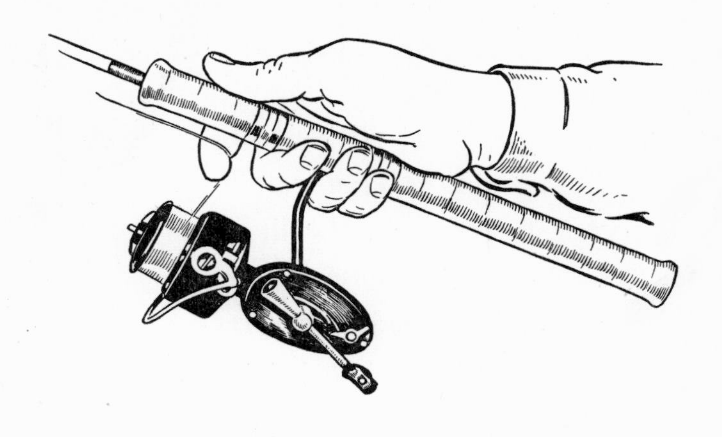

HOLDING SPINNING ROD AND REEL

If you are casting with an open spinning reel, push the bail, or wire, which picks up the line after a cast, out of the way with your left hand. The forefinger of your right hand holds the line after it has been removed from the roller on the reel. The casting weight should hang a few inches from the tip of the rod.

Now hold the rod pointing toward the target and inclined about 15 or 20 degrees. Then bring the rod up and back fast until it is directly above your head. Now start the forward cast immediately. This forward movement is a fast snappy throw. The rod will bend backward. When the rod reaches a position in front of you, release the line from your forefinger and let the casting weight shoot out in front of you. When the weight reaches the spot you want to hit, drop your forefinger on the reel spool to stop the cast.

If you find the casting weight or lure going too high into the air, you released the line from your forefinger too soon. If you wait longer before removing your finger from the line, the weight will travel closer to the ground or water.

Casting with a closed type of reel or spin-casting reel is similar, except that the reel operates differently when releasing or stopping the cast.

If you practice casting with your spinning reel and rod every day for a half-hour or so, in a few days you will have enough accuracy to begin to catch fish.

3 · Bait-Casting Tackle

Rods · Reels · Lines · Leaders · Accessories · How to bait cast

Before spinning tackle became popular, most fresh-water anglers used bait-casting tackle. Casting with a bait-casting reel is more difficult and many fishermen get discouraged; but if you practice long enough you find that this tackle is practical with many types of fishing.

You can cast more accurately with bait-casting tackle than with spinning tackle. This is especially valuable when you fish near shore and have to cast around overhanging trees or near stumps, lily pads, and other tight spots. Bait-casting tackle is also better for hooking and holding big fish such as pike, muskellunge, or lake trout. Using it, you can turn a big fish away from obstructions in the water more successfully. Finally, bait-casting tackle is better than spinning tackle for trolling.

Rods

Formerly bait-casting rods were made of anything from bamboo to steel, but today the solid and hollow glass rods are the most popular. These rods are from 4 to 6 feet long. The short rods of 4 or 4½ feet are best for casting heavy lures at big fish, since they are stiffer in action and do not bend as much under strain.

The 5- and 5½-foot bait-casting rod is practical for general fishing, if you want only one rod. It is usually called a medium-action rod, and will cast lures from ½ to ¾ ounce—the weight of most lures made for bait casting. This rod can be used for black bass, big trout, pickerel, walleyes, small pike, and muskellunge.

The light-action bait-casting rod is about 6 feet long and casts light lures weighing from ¼ to ½ ounce. This rod is best for the smaller fish, such as trout, bass, and pan fish. However, for catching small fish you are better off with a spinning rod and reel.

Bait-casting rods are usually made in two pieces, either separating into two equal lengths or having a

BAIT-CASTING REEL

one-piece tip and a short handle. The handles have two grips and an offset locking reel seat, a curved dip to accommodate the reel. This makes it easier to reach the line on the reel spool with your thumb to slow it down.

Reels

The reel is the most important item of your bait-casting outfit. A well-made, smooth-working reel allows you to cast easily and smoothly and will last many years. A good bait-casting reel doesn't have to be the most expensive on the market; but the cheap reels which cost less than $5 should be avoided. If you spend about $10 you will get a good reel for your rod.

A bait-casting reel has a revolving spool which turns during the cast. You can control the cast and stop it with your thumb. Most bait-casting reels today also have a level-wind device, a metal finger which moves back and forth in front of the reel, spreading the line evenly as it is wound on the spool. In this way the line never bunches up unevenly on the spool, and you have less trouble in casting. Many bait-casting reels also have anti-backlash devices. These prevent the reel spool from revolving too fast during the cast. Most backlashes or line tangles occur when the spool revolves faster than the line can go out. An anti-backlash device applies tension which slows the spool down.

Most modern bait-casting reels have lightweight spools that do not spin as fast or as long as do heavy spools. This feature helps to prevent line snarls or backlashes.

Lines

Before the synthetic lines were developed, bait-casting lines were made of silk. Today most fishermen use either the braided nylon or braided Dacron lines. They are thin, waterproof, and strong.

Bait-casting lines come on spools of 50 yards each. These are connected, so that if you want to fill your reel with line you can buy two or three spools; but one 50-yard spool is enough line for ordinary fresh-water fishing. However, if you want to cast a long distance, you must fill your reel spool with line. To do this, first wind some old fishing line on the reel spool. Then tie on the new bait-casting line and wind it over the old line, called backing. You can also fill the space under the new line by adding a cork arbor around the reel spool to increase its diameter. Some bait-casting reels come equipped with such arbors.

Bait-casting lines come in different strengths, or tests, ranging from 8 to 25 pounds. The lighter lines, testing 8 or 10 pounds, are used with light-action rods. The best size for the medium-action rod is a 12- or 14-pound test line. For the heavy-action bait-casting rod, and for heavy lures and big fish, a line testing 18 or 20 pounds is used.

When you buy a spool of bait-casting line you must transfer it to the reel. To do this, take the end of the line and run it through the level-winding finger and tie it to the reel spool or around the cork arbor. Then take the spool of line and push a pencil through the hole, which is usually covered by the paper label.

Let another person hold the pencil while you crank the handle of the reel to wind on the line. The person who holds the line and pencil should apply some tension by pressing against the sides of the spool with his hands.

Leaders

Since the lines used in bait casting are easily seen by fish, a leader should be used on the end of the line. For this, nylon monofilament material of about 12- or 15-pound test and 3 or 4 feet long is best. On the end of the leader tie a snap-swivel for changing lures quickly. If you fish mainly for pike or muskellunge, you use a short wire leader with a snap. These two fish have sharp teeth and can bite through lines or ordinary leaders.

Accessories

For bait casting you also need a tackle box to hold lures and other accessories. You can buy a bait-casting tackle box or make your own, following the instructions in Chapter 2.

You will also need a wide landing net if you fish from a boat. Get one with a long handle so that you can scoop up a fish easily and don't have to lean too far over the side of the boat.

You will need a wide variety of the bait-casting lures described in Chapter 6.

How to bait cast

After you assemble your bait-casting rod, reel, and line, and a practice weight, you are ready to cast.

In bait casting, the rod is sighted at the target and held with the reel handles facing up. The weight or lure hangs a few inches from the rod tip and the thumb is held against the reel spool. Now, using only the wrist, bring the rod up and back over your head. Stop the rod when it is almost directly over your head. You will feel the weight or lure bend the rod tip still farther back. Then start the forward cast immediately and bring the rod down in front of you, at the same time removing your thumb from the reel spool to send the lure on its way. As the lure moves out, put your thumb back on the line to regulate the speed of the revolving spool. Too much pressure will slow it down and shorten your cast. Too little pressure may allow the spool to overrun and cause a backlash or snarl. When the lure reaches the target, stop the cast with your thumb.

A good bait caster educates his thumb so that it keeps the spool revolving at the right speed. This takes practice, of course, but after a while it becomes automatic. If you have an anti-backlash device on your reel you can adjust this to help you cast better.

4 · Fly-Casting Tackle

Rods · Reels · Lines · Leaders · Accessories · How to fly cast

Fishing with a fly rod is one of the most enjoyable ways of catching any fish, but especially of catching trout. It is also ideal for pan fish, since even the smallest fish puts up a good fight when caught on a fly rod. Many fresh-water anglers would rather catch one fish on a fly rod than a dozen on any other type of fishing tackle.

Some fishermen hesitate to try fly fishing because they believe it is difficult to learn. This is not true, since you can learn how to cast with a fly rod in a short time, and can start catching fish almost from the beginning. However, it does take time to learn how to use the artificial lures with a fly rod. But if you go fly fishing often, this knowledge and skill will gradually be acquired so that they are like a sixth sense.

Rods

Fly rods are made either from split bamboo or hollow glass. Some expert anglers claim that bamboo fly rods have better action than glass rods, but the beginner is better off if he buys a hollow glass fly rod. It is stronger than bamboo and will last longer. It also requires less care after a fishing trip. Fly rods are thin and flexible, and run from 7 to 9½ feet in length. The short rods are used for small streams, short casts, and small fish. The longer rods are used for big rivers and lakes, long casts, and big fish such as the larger trout, bass, salmon, and steelhead, and for salt-water fishing.

The beginner will find that the shorter, lighter fly rods are easier to cast with for long periods, so the first rod you buy should be 7½ or 8 feet long. Make sure it is a trout fly rod with dry-fly action. Such a rod can be used for many kinds of fly fishing.

Fly rods come in two or three sections. Three-section rods are shorter when taken apart and easier to carry. But two-section rods are only slightly longer and it doesn't matter which one you get.

You can buy a good hollow glass fly rod which

will last you a long time for about $15 or $20. You can also spend a few dollars less and still get a serviceable fly rod; but if you buy too cheap a rod you will become dissatisfied with it after a while. If you buy the best you can afford, you will enjoy using it for many years. Make sure that the fly rod has a rigid case where it can be stored when not in use, since the thin tip section of a fly rod is easily broken. If the fly rod has no such rod case, you can buy one to fit it in any fishing tackle store.

Reels

Fly reels are not used in casting but merely hold the fly line that is not being used. Two kinds of fly-fishing reels are used: the single-action and the automatic types. The single-action reel is light and holds a great deal of line. The line is stripped off the reel by hand and is reeled back by hand. There is a handle for winding the line on the reel. Single-action fly reels are cheap; you can buy one for about $5 which will serve the purpose.

The automatic fly reel is heavier and holds less line than the single-action type. However, it is somewhat easier to use, since the slack line is taken up automatically by pressing a lever. These reels are more expensive than single-action reels, and cost be-

SINGLE ACTION

AUTOMATIC

FLY ROD REELS

tween $8 and $15. It doesn't make too much difference which reel you buy, since the reel isn't as important in fly fishing as the rod or line.

Lines

In bait casting or spin casting the weight of the lure carries the line to the target. In fly casting the weight of the line carries the lure to the target. This makes it very important to get the right size of fly line to fit your fly rod. Fly lines are made of silk or nylon, and are coated with various finishes. There are three kinds of lines used in fly fishing: the level line, the double-tapered line, and the three-diameter line. The level line is of equal diameter along its entire length. This is the cheapest fly line you can buy and a good one for a beginner. It costs about $3 or $4; in addition to being an excellent line for practice casting, it can be used for most types of fly fishing. You can use wet flies, streamers, bucktails, and live bait with this line.

The double-tapered fly line is of equal diameter along the center, becoming thinner toward both ends. This is a good general casting line for all fly fishing, except when you are using big bass bugs. It is used mostly for fishing with dry flies. Its advantage is that the thin, light end of a double-tapered fly line makes less disturbance on the surface of the water. A good double-tapered fly line will cost you between $8 and $10.

The three-diameter fly line is also called the torpedo line, bug-taper line, and weight forward line. This line has a short, light tapered section in front, followed by a heavy section (or head), and then by a long, thinner section of line called the running or shooting line. The principle is that a heavy section near the end of the line carries the thinner section to great distances. The three-diameter fly line is therefore designed for making long casts and for casting heavy or bulky lures such as bass bugs. It is best for casting on big rivers or lakes and for bass-bug fishing. This line is even more expensive and costs about $10.

But if you are just learning how to fly cast you

can buy the cheaper fly line. Fly lines come in different weights or thicknesses to match the rod you are using. If you get too light a line you won't be able to cast any distance. The level fly lines are labeled A, B, C, D, E, F, G, H, and I. The "A" line is the heaviest, and "I" the lightest. For an 8-foot fly rod a "C" fly line will be about right. However, it's a good idea to find out from the manufacturer of your rod which size line is best, or to ask an experienced fly fisherman to help you choose the correct fly line.

The level fly line you buy should be the floating type which stays on top of the water. Some of the cheaper fly lines require steady applications of line dressing to keep them floating, but the better lines today are made to float without dressing.

Leaders

Since fly lines are heavy, easily seen, and fall on the water with some disturbance, they easily frighten fish. You therefore need a nylon leader at the end of the line. Your fly or other lure is then tied to the end of this leader. Nylon leaders come either level or tapered. The level leaders are of equal diameter and strength, and can be used for fly casting with bass bugs or for fishing with live bait. But for casting flies you will need tapered nylon leaders. These are thin at the end where the fly is tied and get heavier toward the end where the line is attached. The leaders come in lengths from 6 to 12 feet. In the beginning you will find it easier to cast with 6- or 7½-foot leaders. After you learn how to cast well, you can use the longer ones.

Nylon leaders can be bought already made up in almost any fishing tackle store. However, if you want to save money, you can buy nylon leader material in coils and tie your own fly-fishing leaders. It is best to buy several coils in different strengths and then tie your own tapered leaders. Usually the tippet, or lightest end, will test 2 or 3 pounds and then increase in strength to 10-pound test at the butt end, where the leader is tied to the line. You can cut about 20-inch lengths of 3-, 6-, 8-, and 10-pound test nylon leader

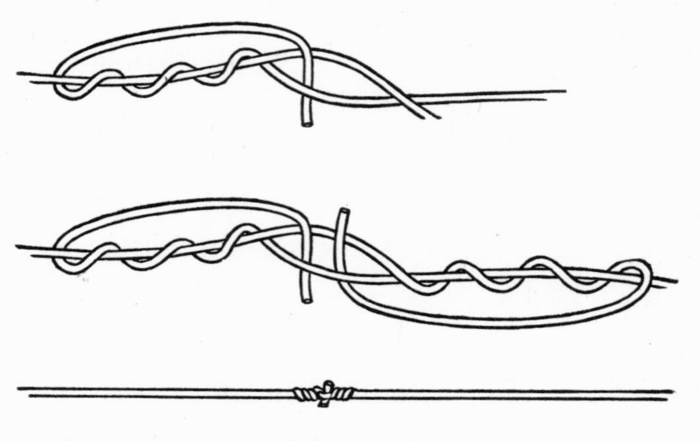

BLOOD KNOT

material and tie them together. This will give you a tapered leader 6 to 6½ feet long. Later you can experiment and tie up different combinations and lengths of leaders to match your fly rod and line and the fishing you do. The best knot for tying nylon leader material together is the blood knot, shown in the drawing. To tie a loop at the thick end of the nylon leader you can use the knot shown in the illustration on page 3.

Accessories

The fly fisherman fishing in streams for trout needs a pair of hip boots or waders. Boots are good enough for small, shallow streams, but for large rivers a pair of waist-high waders is much better. You will

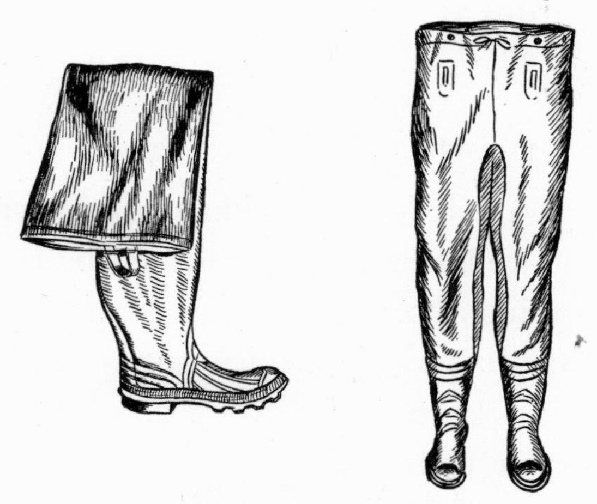

HIP BOOT AND WADERS

also need a creel to keep fish in after they are caught. Two types are made for trout fishermen: the willow creel, which is rather bulky and heavy, and the canvas creel, which is lighter and fits flat against the body.

You also need a light stream-type landing net for netting a trout that has been hooked and brought in close. The best kind of landing net is one with an elastic cord which goes around your shoulder or is attached to a snap on your jacket or vest. As in other types of fishing, you need a small tackle box or two to hold the various artificial flies and other lures. A small transparent tackle box can be used, or one of the small metal fly boxes with separate compartments. To complete the outfit you will need an assortment of artificial flies. These will be described in Chapter 6.

How to fly cast

You can practice fly casting on a lawn or on the water. The rod, reel, and line should be assembled and the fly line threaded through the guides on the rod. Although you can practice casting with the fly line alone, it's a good idea to tie on a 6- or 7-foot tapered leader with a small fly on the end. But clip off the point and barb of the hook on the fly with a

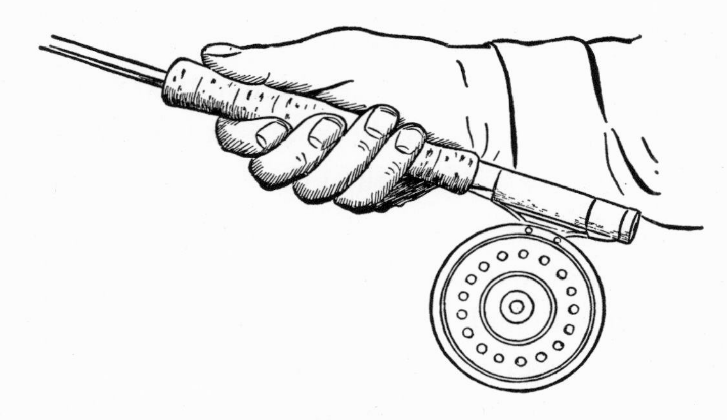

HOLDING FLY ROD

pair of cutting pliers so that you don't get hooked while you are learning how to cast.

Grasp the cork grip on the rod with your right hand, resting the thumb on top. (See illustration above.) Then strip some line off the reel with your left hand and wave the rod forward and backward to let it slip through the guides. Keep the line flying through the air until you have about 25 feet of line past the tip of the rod. Then let it fall in front of you.

When the line is straight in front of you on the lawn or water, point the rod at the target. Now, with a sharp upward and backward motion of your wrist and forearm, pick the line up an let it fly above and behind you, at the same time stripping off more line from the reel. Try to see if you can make the line sail straight up into the air directly above your head. It won't get there, but it will stay high in the air, which is what you want. Stop the rod when it reaches a point at 12 o'clock. The pull of the line will take your rod back a bit more, but don't let it go much farther than a point at 1 o'clock. The line will start unrolling behind you; and, when it is almost straight (you will feel the pull on your rod tip), you start the forward cast. Push the rod in front of you with your wrist. The line will sail forward; follow it with your rod tip.

This is the overhead cast and the one which you will use for most of your fishing. There are other casts which will be easy after you have learned the overhead cast. It takes practice to become a good fly caster, so try to set aside at least a half-hour every day for casting practice.

5 · Fresh-Water Baits

Worms · Minnows · Grasshoppers and crickets · Hellgrammites · Crayfish · Frogs · Other baits

Natural or live baits catch many fish each year in fresh water. A good fisherman must know all about these natural baits: where and how to obtain the bait; how to keep it alive until it is used; how to hook the bait so that it stays alive and attracts fish. Finally he must know how to present the bait to the fish in the best way.

Worms

The most popular bait for fresh-water fishing is the earthworm, or angleworm. Worms are popular because they are usually easy to get and the fresh-water fish bite on them. Two kinds of worms are usually used for fishing. The first is the big night crawler, which may grow to 8 inches in length. It is found in lawns, fields, and gardens, deep in the soil. Night crawlers are too deep to dig out with an ordinary shovel, but they come to the top at night, especially after a heavy rain. You can go out at night with a flashlight and grab them before they can escape into their holes. You have to walk very softly, because these big worms can feel the vibrations through the ground. They are also sensitive to a strong light, so you should shine your flashlight a little to the side of the worm.

The other worm used in fishing is the common earthworm, or garden hackle, which is smaller than the night crawler. It lives in rich, well-moistened soil such as that found in gardens, and can be dug out with a garden fork or shovel. Worms are always easier to find when the ground is wet, since when the ground is too dry the worms burrow deep and are difficult to obtain. Always try to dig your worms after a heavy rain.

When worms are plentiful in the ground it is a good idea to dig as many as you can and obtain enough for several fishing trips. You can keep these worms in a big wooden box filled with earth and rotted leaves. Keep the box in the shade or a cool cellar. The worms can be fed cornmeal, bread crumbs, chicken mash, and almost any other vegetable remains. Mix these into the top of the soil for best results. You can also spill some water over the soil every few days to keep it moist. Worms kept this way in a big box will live for a long time.

When you go fishing you can keep the worms in a small can or box. Fill it partly with earth and put the worms into it. If you keep this container out of the hot sun, the worms will stay alive for an entire day.

There are many ways to put a worm on a hook, depending on what kind of fish you want to catch. When fishing for trout you hook the worm once through the middle. If you are fishing for small pan fish such as sunfish, yellow perch, or rock bass, you

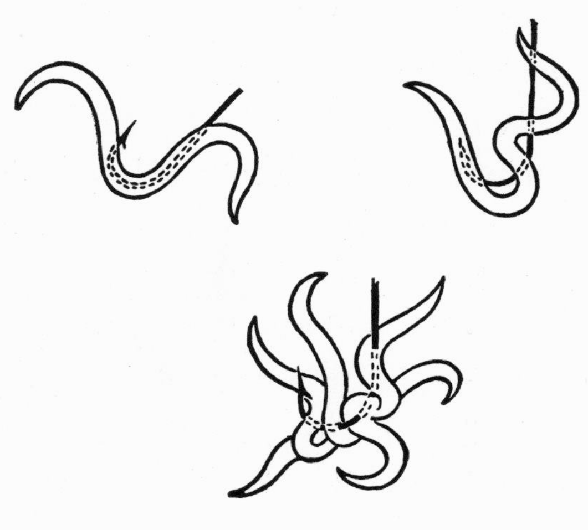

HOOKING WORMS

use small worms, and hook one, two, or three times, allowing both ends to wriggle. For bass one whole night crawler can be hooked once or twice through the middle, or you can put two or three smaller worms on the hook. Catfish and bullheads also like several worms on the hook. (The illustration on the preceding page shows the different ways of hooking worms.)

Minnows

Minnows are small fish which are widely used for bait in fresh water. There are many kinds of minnows, such as chubs, shiners, dace, bluntnose, and fatheads. You can catch your own minnows by using seines, umbrella nets, or minnow traps. A seine is a long net which is dragged through the water by two people. An umbrella net is a square or round net which is tied to strings and is lowered into the water. When the minnows swim into it, it is quickly raised. To attract minnows you can scatter some bread crumbs over the net. A minnow trap is made from wire mesh or glass and has two funnel entrances. Here you also put bread crumbs inside the trap and lower it to the bottom. When the minnows go inside to feed they get trapped and can't come out again.

After you catch the minnows you can keep

MINNOW BUCKET

them alive in a big box made from wire mesh like a cage. This is lowered into the water where the minnows will live for many days. When you go fishing, keep the minnows in a minnow bucket such as the one shown in the drawing. Don't try to keep minnows in an ordinary can or pail: the water will get warm and the minnows will die.

For best results you should use live minnows on the hook. As soon as a minnow dies, take it off the hook and replace it with a live one. You can hook a minnow through the back or through the lips. Small minnows from 1½ to 2 inches long are best for pan fish such as crappies, white bass, and yellow perch; for trout, minnows from 2 to 3 inches long are best; while for bass you can use minnows from 3 to 5 inches in length. For big fish such as pike or muskellunge, minnows or other small fish up to 10 or 12 inches long are sometimes used.

Grasshoppers and crickets

There are many kinds of grasshoppers which can be used as bait in fresh-water fishing. They are found in fields, in gardens, and in the grass and weeds along country roads. You can catch grasshoppers with your hands or by using a small butterfly net. The best time to catch grasshoppers is early in the morning, when the grass is still wet, before the sun gets too high.

Crickets can also be caught in many of the same places where grasshoppers are found. In addition,

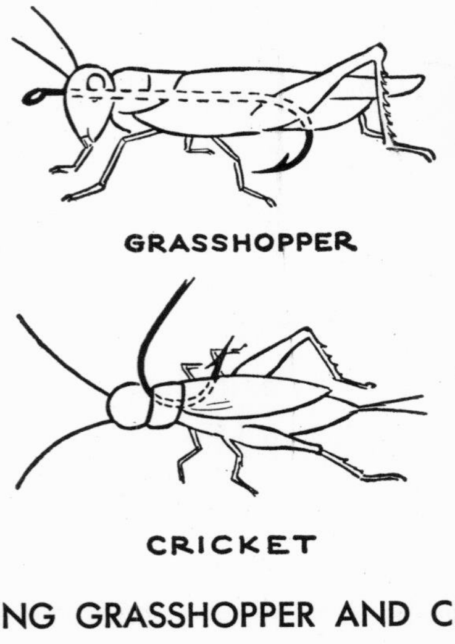

GRASSHOPPER

CRICKET

HOOKING GRASSHOPPER AND CRICKET

they can be found by turning over flat stones, leaves, hay, or any other objects found in the fields.

You can keep both grasshoppers and crickets in a box or other container filled with grass or leaves. The container should have some kind of small opening through which you can remove the insects. For hooking a grasshopper or cricket use a small, fine-wire hook. The illustration shows how to hook a grasshopper and a cricket. These two insects can be used for trout, bass, or pan fish.

Hellgrammites

The hellgrammite is a water insect which later becomes a Dobson fly. It is dark brown or black, with two pincers or nippers and many legs. It grows to be about 3 inches long and lives in many fresh-water streams and rivers. Hellgrammites are also found under rocks in the riffles, or fast shallow waters. All

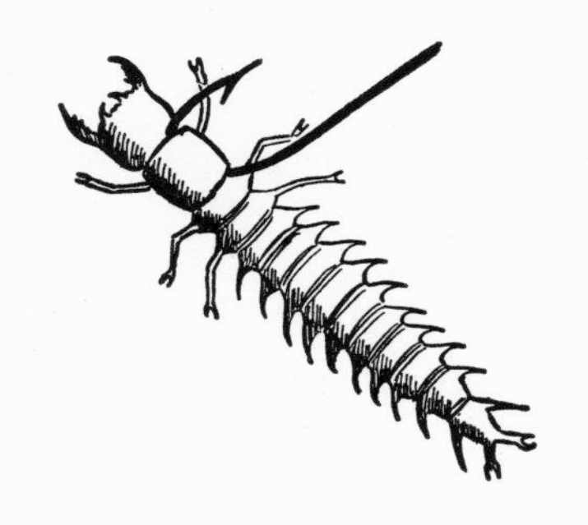

HOOKING HELLGRAMMITE

you have to do to catch them is hold a wire or cloth screen on a wooden frame a few feet below the flat rocks. Then you turn over the rocks and the current will wash the hellgrammites onto the wire screen. You can then remove the hellgrammites from the screen and drop them into a small box or can filled with wet leaves. If you let him, a hellgrammite will bite you with the pincers on his head, but if you grab him by the collar behind his head he can't bite. When you use a hellgrammite, run the hook under this hard collar, as shown in the illustration. He will stay alive a long time on the hook this way. Hellgrammites make good bait for smallmouth black bass, trout, and pan fish.

Crayfish

Crayfish, or crawfish, look like small lobsters and are found in brooks, streams, rivers, and lakes. During the day they hide under stones, around weeds, or in holes in the mud. You can catch them by turning over the stones or poking with a stick in the weeds. Grab them by the back so that they won't be able to bite you with their claws. At night the crayfish come out of their hiding places and are easier to catch, with the help of a flashlight.

After you catch the crayfish you can keep them

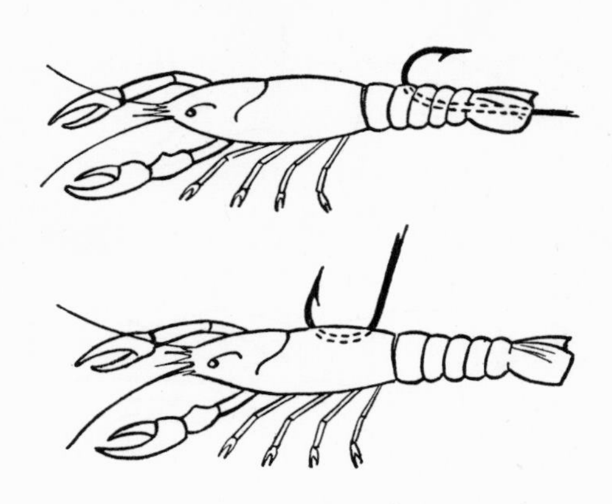

HOOKING CRAYFISH

in a box filled with damp moss or leaves. Crayfish are hooked either through the tail or the back. If you catch a soft crayfish it makes the best bait of all, but it is hard to keep on the hook unless you tie it on with rubber bands or sewing thread. If you use the hard crayfish it is a good idea to break off the two big claws. Crayfish will catch bass, trout, catfish, and other fresh-water fish.

Frogs

Many kinds of small frogs can be used for bait. Green frogs, leopard frogs, pickerel frogs, and small bullfrogs are all good. They are found in the water or on land along the shores of brooks, streams, and lakes. You can catch them by hand or with a small dip net. Keep them in a small wooden box or can

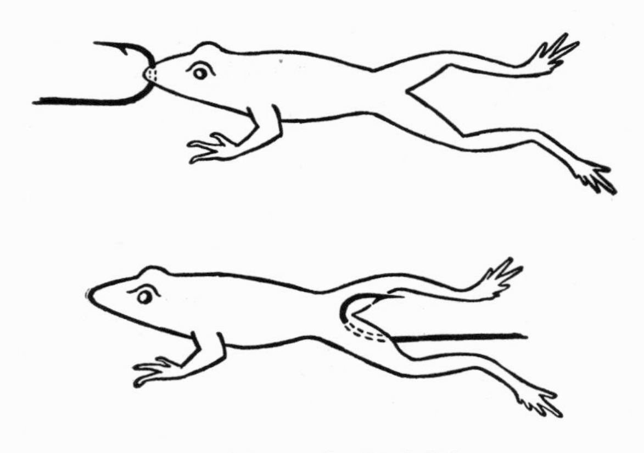
HOOKING FROGS

filled with damp leaves or grass until you are ready to use them. The best way to hook a frog is through both lips. You can also use a special "frog harness," which can be bought in any fishing tackle store.

When using frogs, let them swim around freely on top or under the water. If a fish grabs the frog give him plenty of time to swallow it. Then strike with your rod to set the hook. Frogs will catch bass, trout, pickerel, and pike.

Other baits

There are many other baits you can use when fresh-water fishing. In fact, almost any small worm, insect, or creature which flies, hops, or crawls can be tried for bait. Many kinds of caterpillars make good bait. So do grubs and other small worms found in the ground or in rotten logs. All kinds of beetles and bugs are also eaten by fish. Small lizards or salamanders, which are found in streams or on land, can be used for bait. In the water you'll find small crawling nymphs and larvae which can be put on a hook.

The important thing to remember about using bait is that it should be alive at all times. If the bait dies, take it off the hook and replace it with a live one. And keep your bait moving at regular intervals to attract fish. Bait which doesn't move or hides under a rock or in the weeds won't catch many fish.

Another thing to remember about natural baits is that different states and localities have different laws about catching and using them. Find out from your fishing bureau if the bait you plan to use is legal in your waters.

6 · Fresh-Water Lures

Flies · Bass bugs · Spoons · Spinners · Plugs · Pork rind

Most fishermen agree that using artificial lures is one of the most exciting ways of catching fish. It is also less trouble and cleaner than fishing with natural or live baits. Many anglers dislike handling live baits such as worms, insects, or frogs, and so prefer to use the artificial lures.

The drawback is that there are thousands of artificial lures on the market. When you walk into a fishing tackle store you see so many different lures in various sizes, weights, shapes, and colors that you get confused. Before you can decide which to buy you must learn something about the different lures. Then you can choose a good assortment of lures to use.

Fishing lures are usually designed to look like something fish eat. They represent small flies or insects, bugs, minnows, or other fish, crayfish, frogs, or other small animals. Of course, not all lures look like something to eat. Some of them look strange—like nothing on this earth. Yet they often catch more fish than lures which resemble something alive. That is because fish strike lures for many reasons. Most of the time they grab a lure because they are hungry. But there may be times when they strike a lure because they are curious or angry. Fish can also be very fussy; one day they will take one kind of lure and on the following day they want another kind. So it pays to carry a good assortment of fishing lures on each trip.

Fishing lures fall into many classes, such as flies, bass bugs, spoons, spinners, plugs, and jigs. There are also combinations of all these other lures. We will take them up one by one so that you can become familiar with the best lures to buy and use.

Flies

Artificial flies are made from feathers, hair, fur, wool, tinsel, and other fuzzy materials. These are tied around a hook to look like flies and various insects found above and below the water. We usually

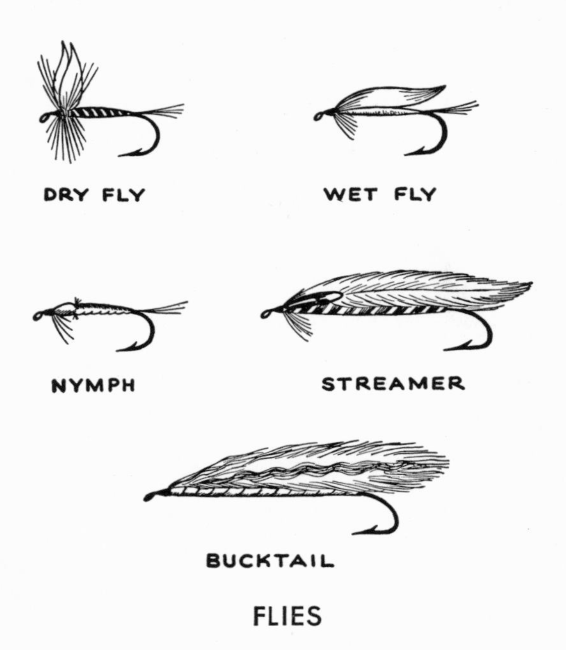

FLIES

divide flies into four classes: dry flies, wet flies, nymphs, and streamer or bucktail flies.

A dry fly is made to float on top of the water. Dry flies have stiff, bulky hackles and tails which support them on the surface, and are tied on thin, light-wire hooks to help them float. Fishermen often apply waterproof fly dressing to keep the fly floating longer. You can buy fly dressing in any fishing tackle store.

There are many different kinds of dry flies. The most common dry fly is called a divided-wing fly and has two erect, separate wings. Other dry flies, the fan wing, spent wing, hackle, variant, spider, and bi-visible, vary somewhat in construction.

Dry flies come tied on different sizes of hooks, usually from number 8 to number 20. The No. 8 is the largest and the No. 20 is the smallest. Sizes 10 to 16 are usually used for trout fishing. There are thousands of different patterns of dry flies, but the following is a good beginners' assortment: Adams, Blue Dunn, Black Gnat, Brown Bivisible, Badger Bi-visible, Light Cahill, Quill Gordon, Hendrickson, Gray Wulff, Brown Spider, and Royal Coachman. These dry flies are good in many parts of the country, but if a good fisherman or the tackle dealer recommends others, include them in your tackle kit too.

Wet flies are made to sink below the surface of the water. They represent an insect which is drowned or struggling under the water. Wet flies are tied on heavy-wire hooks to make them sink faster, and are less bulky than dry flies—a minimum of hair or feathers is used when making them. The standard wet fly has one or two wings, curved low over the body. There are other kinds of wet flies, such as the hackle wet fly, which is sparsely tied and has no wings, and the hair wing, which has wings made of animal hair instead of feathers. Another, the palmer hackle wet fly, has hackle wound around the whole length of the body and resembles a hairy caterpillar.

Most wet flies are tied on hooks from No. 4, the largest, to No. 18, the smallest. The larger sizes are often used when fishing for black bass or big trout; trout fishermen usually get wet flies in sizes No. 8, 10, 12, 14, and 16. As with dry flies, there are thousands of different kinds, but the following is a good assortment to start with: the Dark Cahill, Blue Dunn, Gold-Rib Hare's Ear, Gray Hackle, Quill Gordon, Campbell's Fancy, Parmachene Belle, and the Royal Coachman.

Nymphs are similar to wet flies in that they are also fished under water. They differ in appearance, however, since they usually represent the larvae of various aquatic insects. These insects spend part of their lives under water before they hatch and fly away. While the insect is living in the water it is called a nymph. Nymphs are also tied on heavy-wire hooks from various materials such as feathers, hair, fur, wool, yarn, floss, rubber, plastic, wire, and lead. Most nymphs are drab in color, brown, gray, or black, with light-cream or yellow bellies, and imitate such natural nymphs as the May fly, stone fly, and caddis larva.

The other flies used for trout and bass fishing are the streamers and bucktails. Although they are called flies, streamers and bucktails actually look like small minnows or tiny fish. They are long and are tied on long-shanked hooks. The name streamer is applied to those which have long feather wings. The name bucktail is used for those which have wings of hair, usually the tail of a deer. The bodies of both types are generally silver or gold tinsel. Some of the most popular patterns of streamers and bucktails are the Gray Ghost, Black Ghost, Green Ghost, Mickey Finn, Supervisor, Edson Tiger, and Dark Tiger. Get these in two or three different sizes, such as Nos. 4, 6, and 8.

Flies are used with fly-fishing tackle for trout, bass, pickerel, and pan fish. Some flies are also used in combination with spinners. When you buy flies you should get the more expensive, well-tied flies. Cheap flies are often useless, since they fall apart, do not float and, worst of all, do not catch many fish.

Bass bugs

Bass bugs are similar to flies except that they are usually larger and more bulky, resembling big bugs, beetles, moths, and butterflies. Some are also made to resemble minnows, small fish, and frogs. Bass bugs are fished on the surface of the water with a fly rod, and have bodies made from cork, wood, hair, or

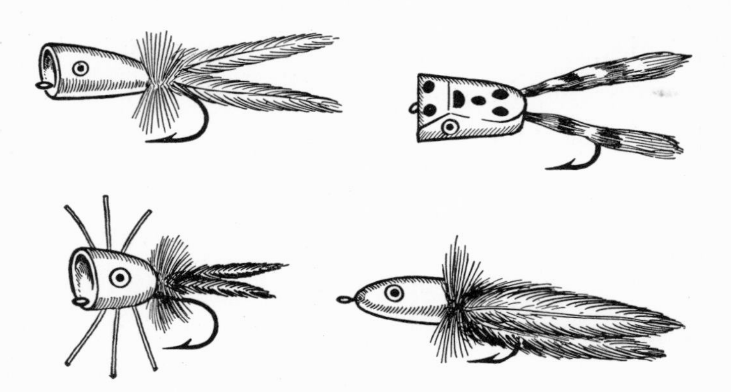

BASS BUGS

plastic, with wings and tails of feathers or hair. (The drawing shows bass bugs of various types.) You should get bass bugs in various sizes and types. The large ones are best for bass. The smaller ones can be used for trout and pan fish.

Spoons

Spoons are among the oldest fishing lures used by man. Spoons made from sea shells and bone were used way back in 3000 B.C. Today most of these lures are made from brass, copper, or stainless steel. Some of them are nickel-plated or chrome-plated to make them silvery. Others are painted in different colors.

Spoons are so called because they resemble a tablespoon with the handle cut off. However, there are many sizes, shapes, and weights. Some are short,

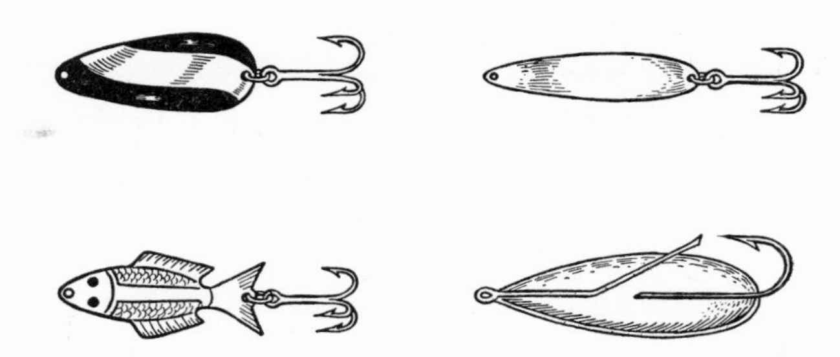

SPOONS

others long and narrow, some oval, others are shaped like small fish. Most of them are bent into a concave or curved shape so that they wobble back and forth in the water. Spoons come with single, double, or treble hooks. The majority have a treble hook attached at the tail end. (The drawing shows different types of spoons.)

You can obtain spoons in different sizes and weights for almost any kind of fishing. There are tiny spoons suitable for use with a fly rod. Spoons of 1½ or 2 inches are best for spinning tackle; larger spoons up to 3 inches are used with bait-casting tackle, while the biggest sizes, up to 5 or 6 inches long, are used when trolling for large fish such as lake trout, pike, and muskellunge.

Spinners

Spinners are somewhat similar to spoons, but they have thin blades which revolve around a wire shaft. These blades come in different shapes, such as oval, egg, willow leaf, and kidney. Spinners usually have one or two blades, but several blades are used for some types of fishing. Some spinners are weighted for casting, while others are used only for trolling. Spinners can have a single hook or a treble hook attached. You can use those with a bare hook by adding a natural bait such as a worm or minnow. Other spinners have flies, pork rind, bucktail, or feathers behind the blade. Spinners come in various sizes, according to the length and width of the blade. Sizes 0 or 1 are the smallest, while size 7 is one of the largest. You should have an assortment of various kinds and sizes of spinners in your tackle box for different kinds of fishing.

Plugs

Plugs are the lures made from wood or plastic to imitate small minnows, fish, frogs, bugs, crayfish, or small animals. There are many different types and shapes on the market in every kind of color and design. You can simplify things by dividing plugs into two classes; these are surface plugs and underwater plugs.

The surface plugs float at rest and travel on top when you reel them in. Most of them cause some kind

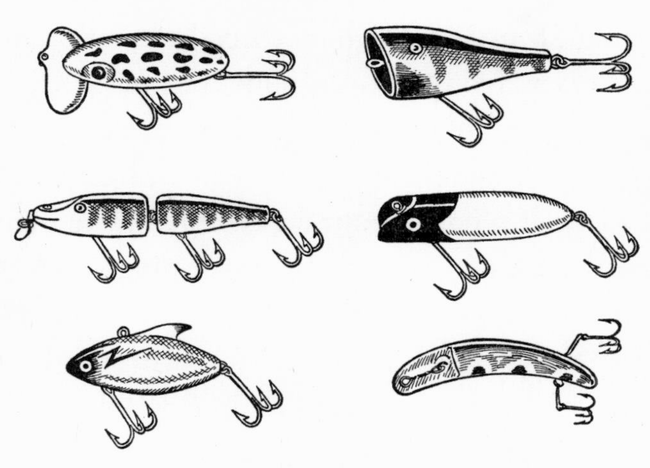

PLUGS

of commotion on top of the water to imitate a crippled fish or other animal. They have cupped heads, metal lips, propellers or other devices for creating a splash or ripple.

The underwater plugs can be subdivided into two classes: those that float on top of the water and then dive when they are reeled in, and those which sink slowly as soon as they hit the water. Most underwater plugs have grooved heads or metal lips which cause them to dive and wriggle like small fish.

Plugs come in different colors, but the most popular finishes are the red-and-white and the natural fish scale. Those that have silver scales are good for many fishes and various waters. Plugs come in different sizes and weights for all types of fishing. Those weighing from ⅛ to ½ ounce are best for spinning tackle. Plugs from ½ to 1 ounce are used for bait casting and trolling and for big fish such as big bass, pike, and muskellunge. It's a good idea to carry an assortment of plugs in your tackle box. (The illustration shows the most popular types of plugs.)

Pork rind

Pork rind, the thick, tough skin from a pig, can be used alone or together with other lures to catch fish. It can be bought in jars in any fishing tackle store. The pork rind comes in strips of varying lengths, widths, and shapes. You can put a strip of

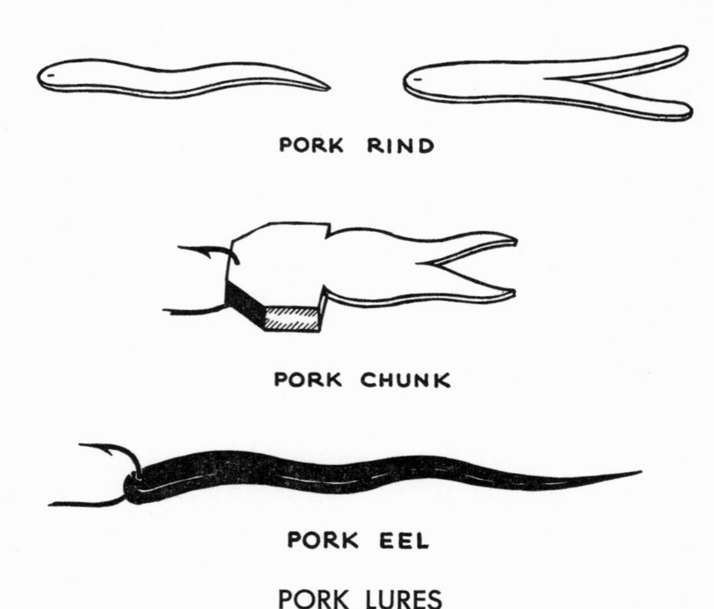

PORK LURES

pork rind on a plain hook and catch fish such as pickerel by skipping it along the surface of the water with a cane pole. Strips of pork rind can also be added to the hooks of spoons and spinners.

Pork chunks also can be used as lures. Here you use the skin as well as some of the fat, cut in the shape of a frog or in a chunk. These are cast around lily pads and worked on the surface for black bass. Pork chunks can also be bought in any fishing tackle store.

Still another pork lure is the black eel strip, which is long, narrow, and dyed black to look like a small eel. They come in two sizes, for spinning or bait-casting tackle. A hook is usually attached at the head of this eel pork strip, which is fished deep, near the bottom. These also come prepared ready for use in jars and are sold by fishing tackle stores.

Pork rind is preserved in a special liquid and should always be put into the jar immediately following use, since it dries out when exposed to air and heat. It weakens with age, and a single strip should not be used more than twice.

7 · Making Fresh-Water Lures

Tying flies · Tying a bucktail · Making a bass bug · Making a spoon · Making a spinner · Making plugs

Most of the artificial lures described in the previous chapter can be made at home. You not only save money by making your own fishing lures, but you have a lot of fun. Making fishing lures also gives you something to do during the long winter months when you are less likely to go fishing. You can make up enough lures during the winter months to last you throughout the fishing season.

Tying flies

To tie your own flies for trout or bass fishing you need a few simple tools which can be bought in many fishing tackle stores: a fly-tying vise, which is specially made for holding hooks when you are tying flies; one or two pairs of fine scissors, with sharp points, in different sizes (you can buy cheap fingernail scissors in any five-and-ten-cent store and they will work, but most fishermen prefer more expensive scissors made especially for fly tying); hackle pliers, which are used to hold the tip of a feather when winding it around the hook; a dubbing needle (this can be bought cheaply, or you can easily make your own—get a large sewing needle and push the end with the eye into a cork bottle stopper); fly-tying silk in sizes oo, ooo and oooo; clear fly-tying cement or clear lacquer.

Of course, you also need many kinds of fly-tying materials such as silk floss, chenille, wool, tinsel, bucktail, squirrel tail, hackle feathers, wing feathers, peacock herl, and peacock sword. And to complete the list you will need an assortment of hooks of various sizes in Model Perfect, Sproat, Limerick, and Humpback patterns.

Instead of buying all these fly-tying tools and materials separately, you can simplify matters by buying a complete fly-tying kit. Such a kit will include all the necessary tools and materials for tying all kinds of flies, and is carried by most fishing tackle stores.

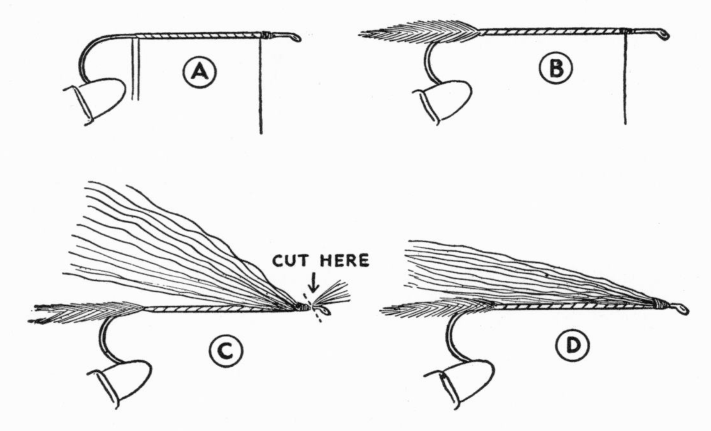

TYING A BUCKTAIL FLY

Tying a bucktail

One of the easiest flies to tie is a bucktail. Place a Limerick or other long-shanked hook in the vise. Then take your fine tying thread and tie it onto the shank of the hook, about ⅛ of an inch behind the eye of the hook. Then tie on the end of the flat tinsel with three extra turns of thread, and wind the tinsel around the hook shank up to the bend. (See *A*.) The tinsel should be wound closely, so that there are no spaces. Now bind on a tail, perhaps two tips of hackle feather, by winding the tinsel around it. Then wind the tinsel back toward the eye of the hook. When you reach the eye of the hook with the tinsel, make one or two turns of thread around the tinsel and then cut off the tinsel. Then make three more turns of thread to cover the end of the tinsel, and bind it off with a half-hitch. (See *B*.) Next you take some white bucktail hair and place it on top of the hook shank and wind several turns of thread around it. Then cut off the ends of the bucktail hair which are protruding over the eye of the hook, cutting at a slant, as shown in *C*. Finish the job by winding thread around the head, tapering toward the eye, and complete the wrapping with a series of half-hitches or a whip finish. See *D* for the finished bucktail fly.

The wet fly, dry fly, and nymph are tied in similar fashion. If you can't find anyone to show you how to tie these flies step by step, buy a book on fly tying. There are several good ones available.

Making a bass bug

To make a bass bug you need a cork body such as a cork bottle stopper. This is then shaped with a razor blade and sandpaper (see page 54). Then you slit the cork lengthwise for a depth of about ⅛ of an inch. You can use a small hacksaw to do this. Now get a hump-shanked hook in size 2/0 and wind two or three hackle-feather points near the bend of the hook. After the feathers are wound in place, continue winding the tying silk along the shank of the hook up to the eye. Finish the wrapping with a series of half-hitches and cut off the thread.

Now get some plastic resin glue, which comes in powder form at any hardware store. Mix it with water, and apply the glue inside the slit in the cork body and around the shank of the hook. You can use a knife blade to work the glue into the slit in the cork. Then force the hook shank into this slit. Wind some thread tightly around the cork body. Now set the cork aside to allow the glue to dry. In the meantime, get some bucktail hair and tie up two wings for the bass bug, cutting the bucktail about an inch and a quarter in length and winding the end with thread. Make two of these. Then take the cork body and make two holes, one on each side, about ¼ of an inch deep, for the bucktail wings. Next force some glue into these holes, applying glue also to the ends of the bucktail wings, and push the wings into the holes. The cork bass bug is now finished except for painting it white, yellow, black, or brown. Use either enamel paint or lacquer, and apply it to the cork body, being careful not to get any paint on the feathers or wings.

Making a spoon

Spoons can be made very easily if you order the finished bodies from a mail-order house, such as

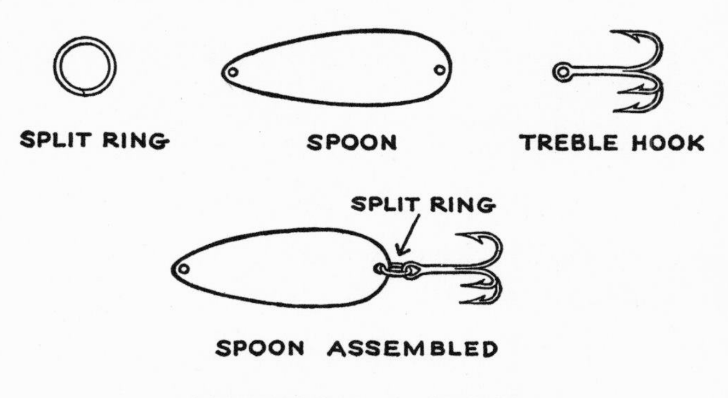

ASSEMBLING A SPOON

Herter's. (The addresses of this company and others are at the end of this chapter.) These companies have all sizes of spoons in various shapes, weights, and finishes. You get the metal bodies and also some split rings and treble hooks. These spoon bodies have two holes, one on each end. Take a knife blade and spread two split rings, forcing one into each hole. Then force the treble hook onto the tail end of the spoon. The different parts of a spoon and how they are assembled are shown in the illustration above.

Making a spinner

The parts needed to make a spinner can also be obtained from a mail-order supply house. To make a complete spinner you will need blades, beads, clevises, stainless-steel wire, and hooks. The most popular spinner blade is the Indiana type, in nickel-

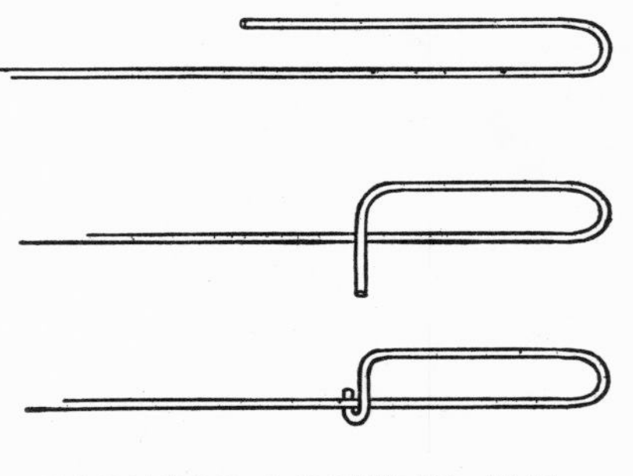

FORMING LOCKING EYE

plated finish. You can get this blade in different sizes to make spinners for all your fishing needs.

To make a simple spinner, cut an 8-inch length of size 10 stainless-steel wire. Then form a locking eye on one end of this wire. To cut the wire use diagonal cutting pliers. To form the locking eye use round-nose pliers. The drawings above show how to form this eye. After the locking eye is finished get four to six beads and slip them on the wire so that they rest against the locking eye. Then put a spinner blade on the clevis and slide the clevis on the wire shaft through the two holes. To finish the spinner, form another eye on the end of the wire to take the line. The finished spinner will look like the one in the illustration. This type of spinner is best for trolling, but if you add a clincher sinker to the leader or line it can also be cast. To use this spinner all you have to do is add a single hook to the locking eye. You

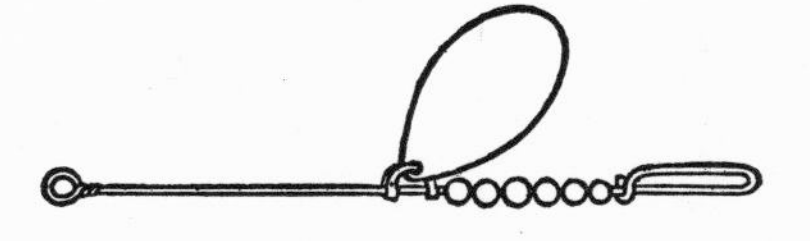

FINISHED SPINNER

can put a worm, a strip of pork rind, or a minnow on this hook. Instead of a bare hook you can also add a treble hook with bucktail or feathers, or you can attach a big bass bug to the locking eye.

Making plugs

To make plugs for fresh-water fishing you need some kind of wood which can be worked easily with hand tools such as a knife, saw, file, and wood drill. Almost any wood can be used to make plugs, but woods such as cedar, birch, and basswood are best, since they are light, float well, and are easy to carve. Such woods are sold in many lumberyards. You can start with a block of wood and whittle a plug with a sharp knife. Or you can put the block of wood in a vise and use a rasp to form the plug. Then you can use a smooth wood file and sandpaper to finish it off.

However, you can save all this work if you order the ready-shaped wood or plastic bodies from a supply house. These bodies come finished except for the hardware, which is added to them. To com-

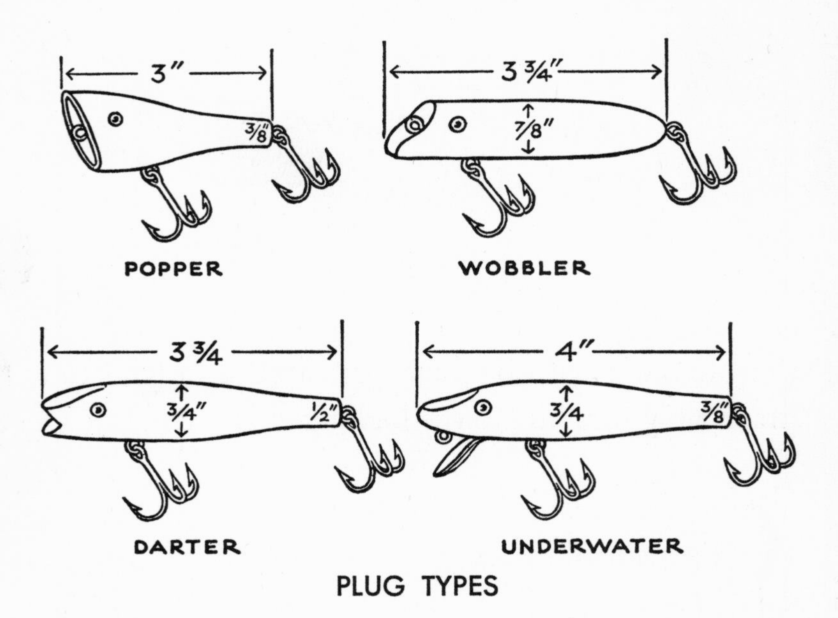

PLUG TYPES

plete a plug, you need screws, screw eyes, and treble hooks.

The four basic fresh-water plugs you can make easily are shown in the drawing above. The first plug shown is the popper type, which can be 3 inches long and 1 inch in diameter at the wide end. The tail end tapers to a diameter of ⅜ inch. The face of the plug is carved like a dish or cup so that it will throw water when jerked.

The second plug you can make is the wobbler type, which is about 3¾ inches long and ⅞ inch wide. It tapers to a point at the tail. The head of this plug is cut at an angle and can be grooved.

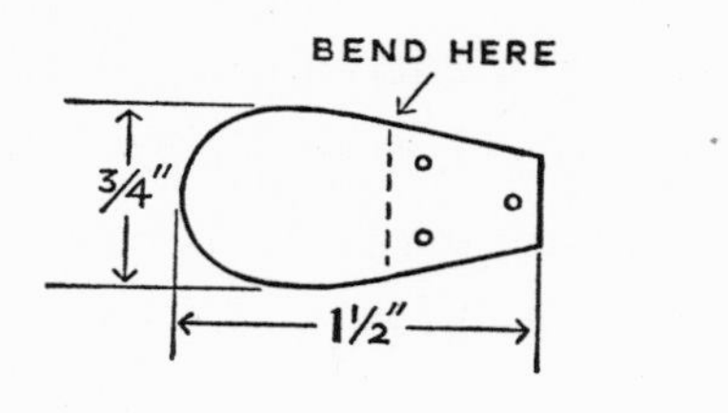

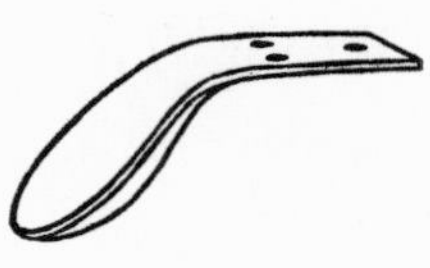

METAL LIP

The next plug is the darter type, which is also 3¾ inches long and ¾ inch in width. A notch is cut in the head, and the top of the head is filed, as shown in the drawing.

Finally we have the underwater plug, which is 4 inches in length and ¾ inch wide. This plug tapers toward the tail, where it is ⅜ inch wide. For this plug you will need a metal lip, which is screwed in under the plug near the head. You can cut such a lip from sheet metal of brass, copper, or aluminum. Bend it as shown and give the lip a shape like a shallow cup, using a ball-peen hammer. Then drill three holes in the metal lip and screw it on the plug body. Finished, ready-to-use metal lips can also be ordered from a mail-order house.

The sizes above are suggested for bait-casting plugs which must weigh at least ⅝ ounce. But you make them smaller and lighter for use with spinning tackle.

The plugs are assembled by screwing in the

treble hooks. A screw eye is opened and the hook eye slipped into it. Then it is closed, and the screw eye is screwed into the wooden body of the plug. Use an awl or ice pick to make a hole in the wood to get the screw eye started.

After the plugs have been assembled they should be painted with enamel or lacquer. Lacquers dry faster but do not give as smooth a finish as enamels. If you have an airbrush, you can spray lacquers and do a good job. You can also buy a can of pressurized spray paint and spray the plugs white or silver. No matter what color you paint the plug finally, you should give it at least two coats of white paint first to waterproof the wood. Then you can add any other colors you want.

The following mail-order companies sell parts and materials for tying flies or making fishing lures. Write them for their catalogs:

Herter's, Inc., Waseca, Minnesota
Netcraft Co., 3101 Sylvania Ave., Toledo, Ohio
Reed Tackle, Box 390, Caldwell, New Jersey

8 · Fresh-Water Fish

Trout · Black bass · Pan fish · The pike family · Walleye · Catfish · Carp

Trout

The trout family are among the most popular fish caught in fresh water. These fish, which are found mostly in cold-water streams, rivers, and lakes, are all noted as great fighters on the end of a line. Trout are also highly prized because they make particularly good eating.

There are many different kinds of trout found in the United States and Canada. The most popular varieties are described here.

The brook trout is often called the native trout because it was the only trout found in the northeastern part of the United States when the first white settlers arrived. Later, brook trout were introduced

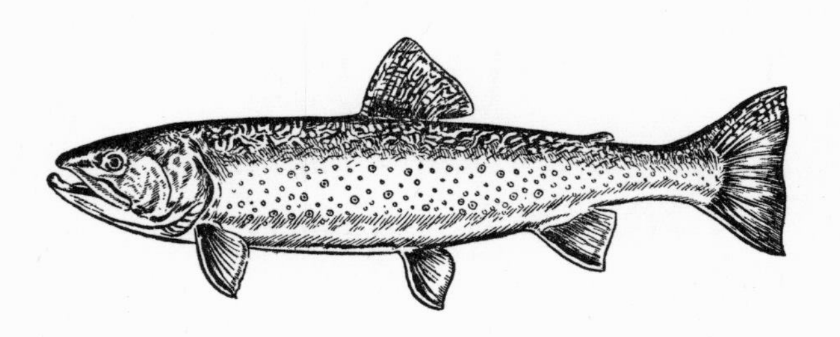

BROOK TROUT

in the West, and today they are found mostly in the northern part of the United States and Canada. They are also called mountain trout, brookie, speckled trout, and squaretail.

Brook trout like clean, cold water, and are most numerous in the smaller, spring-fed streams in mountain and wilderness areas. They often live in tiny feeder streams that are so narrow that you can step across them. But in Canada and other northern areas they are often found in large rivers and lakes.

The average brook trout is on the small side when caught, weighing ½ to 1 pound. However, in some of the larger rivers and lakes, they may reach a bigger size. The world's record brook trout caught on rod and reel was caught in the Nipigon River in Ontario, Canada, and weighed 14½ pounds.

The brook trout is a beautiful, brightly colored fish, with a speckled back, red spots, and pink fins edged with white.

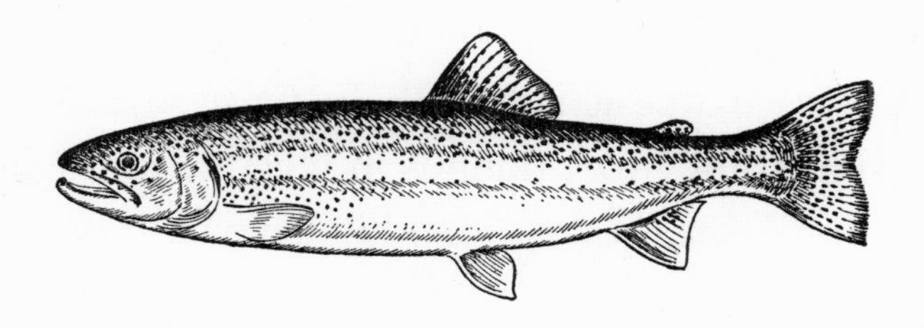

RAINBOW TROUT

The rainbow trout is another handsome, hard-fighting favorite with fly fishermen. It grows larger than the brook trout and is most common in the West, where it is native; but rainbow trout have also been introduced into many other waters of the northern United States.

You can usually identify rainbow trout by the black spots all over the body and fins, and also by the pink or purplish-red band which runs along the sides of the fish from the head to the tail.

Rainbow trout are found mostly in the faster portions of the larger streams, rivers, and lakes. They like to migrate or travel, and swim up and down streams and rivers entering lakes or the ocean. Some rainbows on the Pacific Coast migrate to the sea and are then called "steelhead." After living in the sea for a while, they change color and become steel-blue and silvery in appearance. The spots and pink band fade and become less noticeable.

The size of the rainbow caught will depend on the waters where it is found. In most small streams they run from ½ to 5 pounds in weight. In the larger rivers and lakes they reach a bigger size. The largest caught on rod and reel weighed 37 pounds.

At one time there were no brown trout in the United States. Then some brown-trout eggs were imported from Europe, and the young trout were planted in waters all over the United States, so that today they are numerous in most of our northern states and parts of Canada.

The brown trout can stand warmer waters than either the brook or rainbow trout. It is also a harder fish to catch and can survive in streams that are heavily fished. Because of this you will find that most of the trout found in streams near our larger cities are the smart brown trout.

Brown trout are so called because they are dark brown on the back, blending into a lighter brown on the sides. They also have black, brown, and red spots on the back and sides.

The brown trout reaches a big size in the larger rivers and lakes, where the biggest ever caught on rod and reel weighed 39½ pounds. However, in most streams and lakes brown trout will run from 1 to 8 pounds in weight.

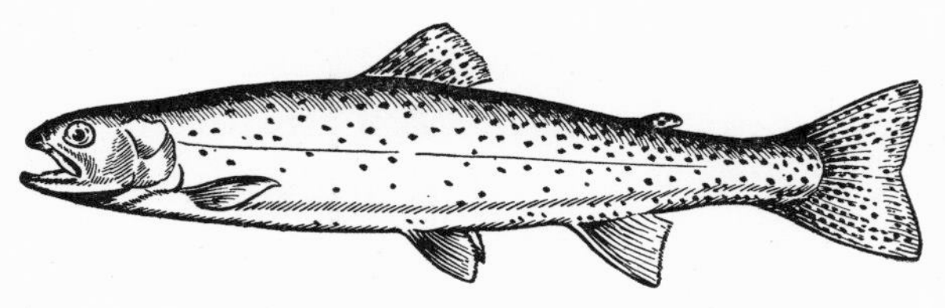

CUTTHROAT TROUT

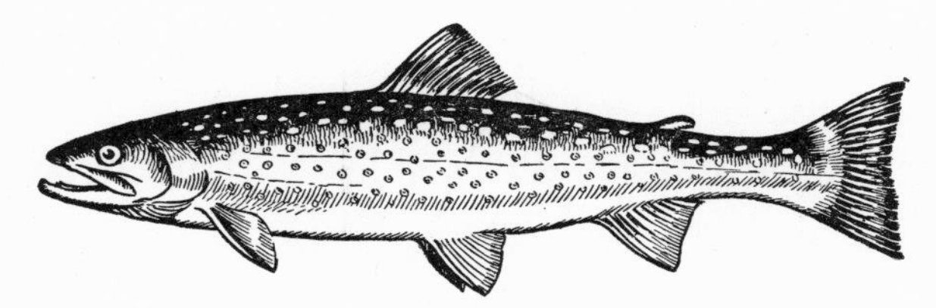

DOLLY VARDEN TROUT

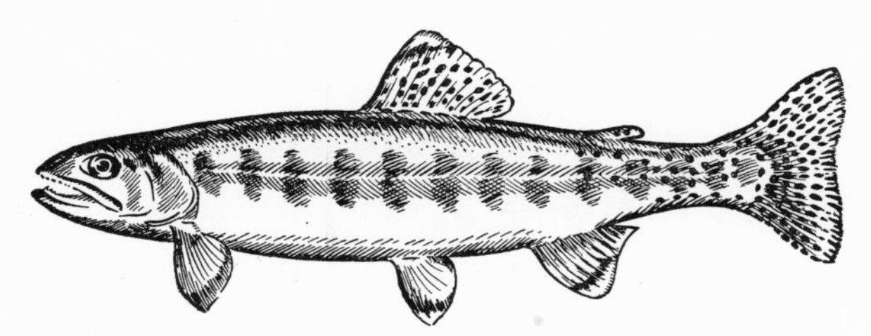

GOLDEN TROUT

Some of the other trout caught include the cutthroat, Dolly Varden and golden trout. The cutthroat trout gets its name from the red streak on both sides of the lower jaw. It is found from California to Alaska along our Pacific Coast and also in the Rocky Mountains. Cutthroat trout usually weigh from 1 to 6 pounds, but the world's record is 41 pounds.

The Dolly Varden trout is another which is

common in western waters, where it is found from California to Alaska. It has red and orange spots on the body, and the lower fins are edged with white, like those of the brook trout. It can grow to 29 pounds in weight, but in small streams and rivers it runs from ½ to 5 pounds.

The golden trout is the most beautiful trout of all, with its golden-yellow sides and its bright red stripe running midway along its body from head to tail. Over this there are dark blotches spaced at regular intervals, usually numbering about ten. This trout is found in only a few places in the West, such as the Sierras of California. It rarely reaches more than a pound in weight in the smaller streams. The largest golden trout caught on rod and reel weighed 11 pounds.

In general, you will find the best trout fishing in the spring and early summer. The months of May and June are usually good. However, if the water isn't too low or warm, you can often have good fishing during the summer months as well. But usually during the summer the trout fishing is good only early in the morning, in the evening, and at night. Later the fishing is often good again during September and October.

The most difficult part of trout fishing is locating the fish in a stream or lake. Most beginners who go trout fishing concentrate their fishing on the larger pools because of the deeper water. They feel that such spots have more fish. While it is true that pools often contain many trout, these fish are usually resting and are therefore difficult to catch. When trout are actively feeding they will come into shallow and fast water provided that there are places such as deep holes, rocks, ledges, and logs where they can lie hidden and protected from the full force of the current. Early in the morning and in the evening, trout will often be found at the tail end of pools and in the fast water. Trout usually face upstream and watch for food being swept their way by the current.

When you fish for trout always approach the water carefully. Avoid casting shadows over the water, walk lightly along the bank, and avoid bumping into rocks when wading. You may even have to hide behind a bush if the water is shallow and clear. In small streams it is best to stay out of the water, since any disturbance will frighten the trout. If you do frighten the trout, give the spot a rest for at least half an hour before you fish it again. Fish slowly and don't be afraid to make several casts in a spot which looks good.

In lakes, trout often stay close to shore, where

they can be caught around rocks, logs, overhanging trees, and weeds. They also gather at spots where brooks, streams, or rivers enter the lake. In the summer months trout stay deep and near underwater springs.

When using dry flies for trout in a stream, wade upstream, casting the fly into likely-looking spots slightly upstream and out from where you are standing. Then let the current take the fly downstream as naturally as possible. If the fly starts to drag unnaturally, lift it from the water and make a new cast. Dry flies are best when there are many insects hatching or flying over the water and you see trout feeding on them. But you can also catch trout by casting blindly and hoping that a fish will see the fly and come up for it.

When using wet flies, cast the sinking fly slightly upstream, a few feet above the spot you want to fish. Then you let the fly sink and float downstream into the best spots. You can let the fly drift naturally without any rod action or you can retrieve the wet fly in short jerks.

Nymphs are used somewhat like wet flies in that they are cast up or across the stream and are allowed to sink and drift with the current. Then, when the nymph completes its drift and the line starts to straighten out, you can retrieve it upstream in short jerks. It is important to watch the leader and line carefully for any indication of a strike when fishing with nymphs or wet flies. Sometimes you will see the trout flash under the water as it grabs the lure. Then you should strike immediately to set the hook.

When you use bucktails or streamers you can cast them across stream or downstream. Then retrieve the fly rapidly in short jerks to imitate a frightened or crippled minnow or other small fish.

In large streams and rivers you can also use a spinning outfit or a bait-casting outfit to catch trout. Then you cast such lures as spoons, spinners, and small plugs, retrieving them by reeling in at various speeds.

Trout can also be caught on natural baits such as worms, minnows, and grasshoppers, or other insects. A fly rod can be used with these, since you can cast these baits better and control them in the water. Worms and minnows are especially good baits to use early in the year when the trout season opens and the trout are feeding deep below the surface. Live insects are better later on, during the late spring and summer, when they are naturally eaten by trout. When using natural baits it is important to keep them moving. Let the worms and minnows drift naturally with the current, as if they had no line attached. You don't have to strike immediately when a trout takes a natural bait. Instead, give him time to swallow it before you try to set the hook.

Black bass

The black bass is the favorite fresh-water game fish in the United States. More fishermen like to fish for bass than any other true game fish. They are more plentiful and found in more areas than trout: almost every large lake or river contains black bass. Most of the fresh-water fishing tackle, such as spinning and bait-casting rods and reels, are designed to catch bass. And hundreds of lures, such as spinners, spoons, plugs, and jigs, have been made especially for black-bass fishing.

This popularity of the black bass is well deserved, since it is a true game fish in every way. They put up a stubborn fight on the end of the line, often leaping out of the water or standing on their tails to shake their heads. Black bass are smart fish and soon learn to avoid lures and baits which are carelessly presented, but will strike well-presented artificial lures regularly. In almost every lake you'll find big, wise black bass which are hard to hook. This makes black-bass fishing a challenge, and if you can catch these fish with some regularity you can consider yourself a good fisherman.

There are several species and sub-species of black bass found in the United States. But fishermen are most familiar with the largemouth bass and the smallmouth bass. The largemouth bass is also called the bigmouth bass, grass bass, green bass, straw bass, bayou bass, slough bass, lake bass, marsh bass, and linesides. It is pale green along the sides of the body, with a dark-green back, and a black stripe running along the sides in the center, starting at the head and ending at the tail. This black line is sometimes faint but is usually quite distinct and can be seen on a fish in the water many feet away. Finally, the largemouth bass has an upper jaw which extends beyond its eye, from which it gets its name.

Largemouth bass are found in almost every state in the country and in parts of Canada. They prefer the warmer lakes, slower rivers, ponds, and other

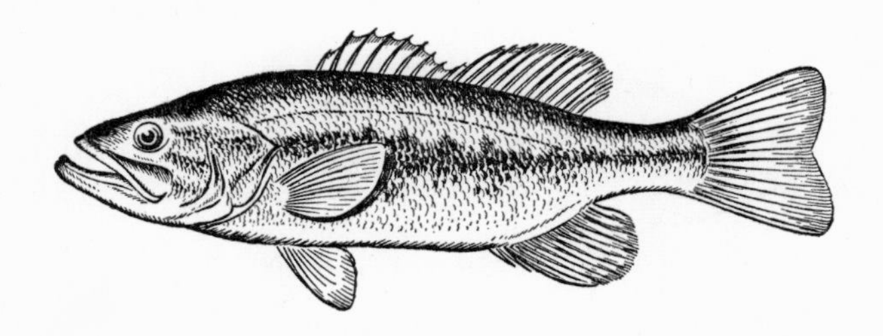

LARGEMOUTH BASS

waters where lily pads, weeds, and other vegetation are plentiful.

Most of the largemouth bass caught will weigh from 1 to 5 pounds. In southern waters, such as the Florida lakes, bass often reach 10 pounds or more. The largest one ever caught came from Montgomery Lake in Georgia, and weighed 22 pounds, 4 ounces.

The smallmouth bass is more bronze or brassy-green in color. It has brown or bronze vertical lines on the sides, running from the back to the belly. The jaw of the smallmouth bass doesn't extend beyond its eye when the mouth is closed.

Smallmouth bass are found in many of the same areas as the largemouth and are most plentiful in northern areas and in Canada. They are rare or absent in most of our southern states. They are usually found in colder, faster, and cleaner water than the large-mouth bass, especially lakes with sand, gravel, or rock bottoms, or streams with fast currents.

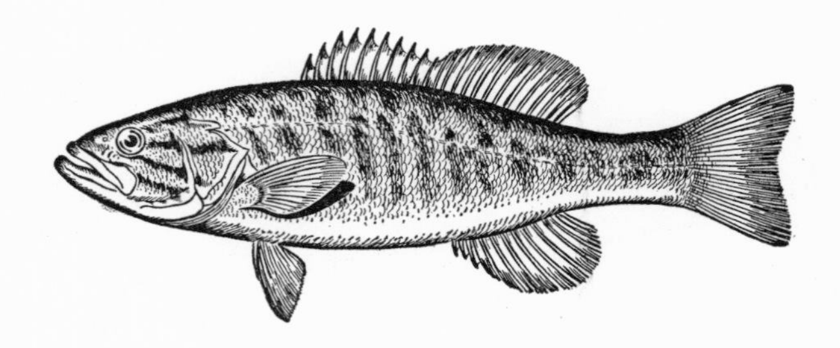

SMALLMOUTH BASS

Smallmouth bass do not reach as large a size as the largemouth. The average fish caught runs from 1 to 3 pounds. The largest caught weighed 11 pounds, 15 ounces and was caught in Dale Hollow Lake, in Kentucky and Tennessee.

Largemouth bass are found in many parts of a lake, depending on the season, the temperature of the water, and the type of food present. In the late spring and early summer, when the water warms up, bass move close to shore into shallow water. They stay there to feed and spawn until the water gets too warm. Then they go back to deep water again, especially during the daytime. However, in the evening, at night, and early in the morning, bass often come back to the shallows to feed. So the general rule during the hot summer months is to fish near shore early in the morning and at night and in deeper water during the daytime.

Largemouth bass in a lake are usually found around lily pads, hyacinths, and other plants. Sunken trees, logs, and stumps in the water also attract them. In deeper water look for underwater weed beds, where bass will often gather in schools.

Smallmouth bass in a lake prefer spots with sand, gravel, or rock bottoms. Deep water along rocky shores and cliffs, gravel or rock bars which drop off into deeper water are favorite hangouts for these fish.

Smallmouth bass are also found in rivers and streams. Here they stay in the deeper pools and eddies most of the time, but at times they will come into the fast rapids or riffles to feed, and can be caught there. They usually stay close to large rocks or boulders in rivers.

One good method of fishing early in the morning or in the evening when bass are in the shallows is to row around a lake about 50 feet from shore. Here you usually need two people, one to row the boat and another to cast toward shore. You can use either a spinning or a bait-casting rod for this type of fishing. The best lures to use are usually surface plugs such as the poppers and crippled minnows. Cast the plug as close to shore as possible, or else near a stump, log, or lily pad. Then let the plug lie there for about a minute or so. Next you twitch the plug or pop it and let it lie still again. Move or pop it again and let it stay in one place once more. Keep doing this until the plug has almost reached the boat, making the plug imitate a frog or crippled minnow that can't swim too fast.

Some surface plugs have metal lips or wings which create a commotion or fuss on top of the water.

These can be reeled steadily at any speed. Try reeling slowly first, then faster on the next cast.

Underwater plugs are also good lures for bass. Some of these float on top of the water, then dive and travel just below the surface. These can be used close to shore, where the water is shallow. But when the bass are in deep water, as is often the case in the middle of the day during the summer, then deep-running underwater plugs or sinking plugs must be used. The closer you can get to the bottom with underwater plugs the better your chances are of catching fish.

Plugs that sink are fished close to the bottom simply by letting them go down. When such a plug hits bottom, reel it slowly a few feet, then let it pause or sink again, then reel it once more, and keep doing this until the plug is near the boat.

Another good lure when the bass are down deep is the black pork eel. Let this also sink to the bottom, then raise it a few inches and let it sink once more, giving it a lifelike action. Rubber worms can also be used in the same way.

You can also catch bass on spinners and spoons by casting and reeling in at various speeds. For best results try an erratic retrieve with regular sweeps and jerks of the rod tip. Spoons and spinners are especially good lures for smallmouth bass in rivers, since they sink fast in the current and reach the fish deep down.

Bass are often caught trolling in a lake or river. Here you let the lure out behind the boat and run the outboard motor at a fairly slow speed. The best speed is usually the one which brings the proper action out of a fishing lure. Such lures as underwater plugs, spoons, spinners, and flies, or spinners and bait can be used when trolling. In trolling you let out anywhere from 50 to 150 feet of line behind the boat. Usually the more line you let out the deeper the lure will travel.

Another way to catch bass is with a fly rod and flies or bass bugs. Bass bugs are especially good lures when used with a fly rod. You can also use some of the weighted bass bugs with a light spinning rod. When using bass bugs, fish them very slowly near shore or in shallow water. Cast out and let the bug lie on top of the water for a minute or more. Then give it a few short jerks or twitches and let it lie still again. Continue doing this until the bug is near you, then cast to another spot and repeat the retrieve.

Bass can also be caught on other fly lures, such as streamers, bucktails, and wet flies. These lures are especially good for smallmouth bass in streams and rivers, which are fished in much the same way as described in the chapter on trout fishing.

When bass refuse to take artificial lures they can often be caught on natural baits such as minnows, worms, frogs, hellgrammites, crayfish, and insects.

Minnows can be used in a lake with or without a float. If there are a lot of weeds it is better to use a small float, but in open water you can use a minnow alone. Hook the minnow through the lips or back and let it swim around. When you see the float go down or move away, do not strike immediately but wait a few seconds until the bass has a chance to swallow the small fish. Then, when he starts moving away once more, set the hook. Frogs can be fished the same way—give the bass plenty of time to swallow the bait before striking.

Either the large night crawlers or the small worms can be used for bass if you put two or three or more worms on a hook. Bass like a lot of worms wriggling, so keep changing the worms if they die. Worms can be fished with a float suspended in the water, or you can use them without a float and let them sink to the bottom. In a stream you can also either let the worms drift naturally with the current or go down to the bottom.

Hellgrammites and crayfish can also be fished

with or without a float. In lakes it is usually best to use a float, while in streams and rivers it is best to let these baits sink to the bottom or drift with the current.

When fishing for black bass you must use your imagination and experiment with various lures and baits until you find what your fish want. That is why the best bass fishermen usually carry a great assortment of lures with them on every trip.

Pan fish

The so-called "pan fish" are several small fish which are caught in fresh-water lakes and rivers. They include such fish as the sunfish, rock bass, crappies, yellow perch, white perch, and white bass. These small fish are not only good for the pan or eating, but also provide good sport with a light fishing outfit such as a fly rod or spinning rod.

SUNFISH

The largest and most popular sunfish is the bluegill. This sunfish is found in many parts of the United States, and it is often stocked in newly built farm ponds. The bluegill is recognized by the black blotch found on the back edge of the gill cover. This sunfish averages from 6 to 8 inches in length and about half

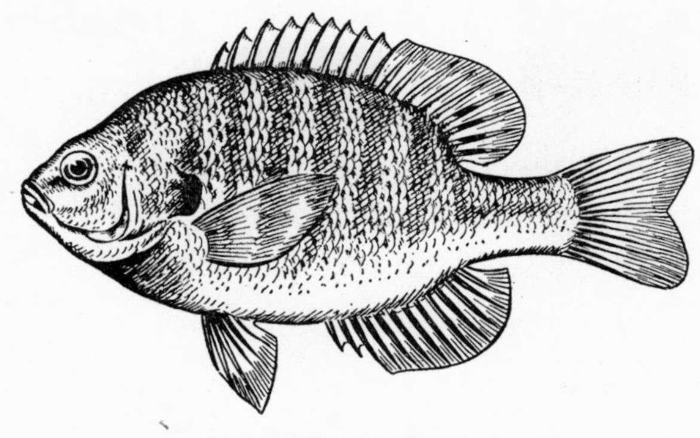

BLUEGILL SUNFISH

a pound in weight, although from time to time big ones weighing 1, 2 or even 3 pounds are caught. The largest ever caught on rod and reel weighed 4 pounds, 12 ounces.

Another popular sunfish is the pumpkinseed, or common, sunfish. This sunfish doesn't grow as big as the bluegill, rarely reaching more than a pound in weight. Most of them run up to 5 or 6 inches in length. This sunfish is most numerous east of the Mississippi River but has also been stocked in some western states.

Other sunfish are the green, long-eared, red-breasted, warmouth, and shell-cracker, or red-eared, sunfish. Sunfish are known by many names in various areas and are often called bream in the South. Most sunfish feed on small minnows, worms, grasshoppers, crickets, snails, beetles, and other insects.

ROCK BASS

The rock bass is related to the sunfish and is often called redeye or goggle-eye. This pan fish is bronze or olive-green in color and has a red eye.

Rock bass are found mostly in the eastern and midwestern United States. They live in rivers and lakes, preferring the quieter and deeper parts of streams and rivers.

The average size of the rock bass caught is about ½ pound, but they reach up to 2 pounds.

CRAPPIES

The crappie is another fish which is related to the sunfish, with a similar flat and deep body. There are two kinds of crappies, the white crappie and the black crappie. They look very much alike; the only way to tell the difference is to count the dorsal spines.

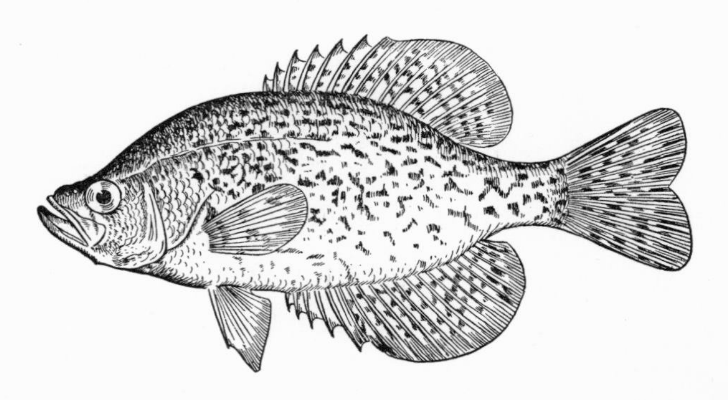

CRAPPIE

The white crappie has 5 to 7 spines in the dorsal fin, while the black crappie has 7 or more. Both crappies are a pale yellow and light green along the back, with irregular dark spots on their silver sides and belly.

Both species are found in many parts of the country; but the black crappie is most plentiful in the North; the white crappie, in the South.

Most crappies caught weigh ½ to 1 pound, but sometimes they reach as many as 2 or 3 pounds. The largest crappie caught weighed 5¼ pounds. This was a white crappie, which is larger than the black.

YELLOW PERCH

The yellow perch is another pan fish which is very popular with fresh-water anglers. It is easily recognized by its dark olive-green back and stripes over golden-yellow sides.

At one time the yellow perch was found only

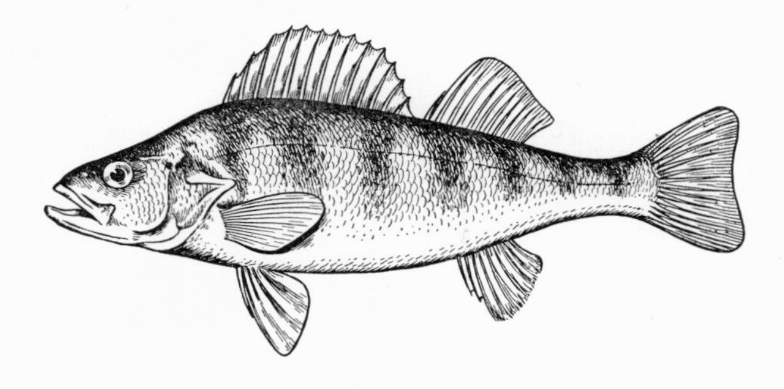

YELLOW PERCH

in the eastern part of the United States, from Canada to North Carolina, but it has since been stocked in many other parts of the country.

The yellow perch prefers water somewhat colder and deeper than other pan fish like, and so is most plentiful in our northern lakes and rivers.

Most yellow perch run from about 8 to 10 inches in length, depending on the waters in which they are found. In some lakes yellow perch never reach a big size, while in others large perch are common. The largest yellow perch ever caught weighed 4 pounds, 3½ ounces.

Yellow perch are considered one of the tastiest pan fish in fresh water. For eating purposes, in fact, many anglers prefer them to bass or even trout.

WHITE PERCH

This pan fish is not a true perch but belongs to the bass family. White perch have an olive or dark-green back and silvery sides, and are shaped like the yellow perch. It is a pan fish which is caught along the Atlantic Coast from Nova Scotia to South Carolina. The white perch can live in salt or brackish water—in fact it prefers rivers which enter the sea. But it can also live in fresh-water lakes if trapped or stocked in such waters.

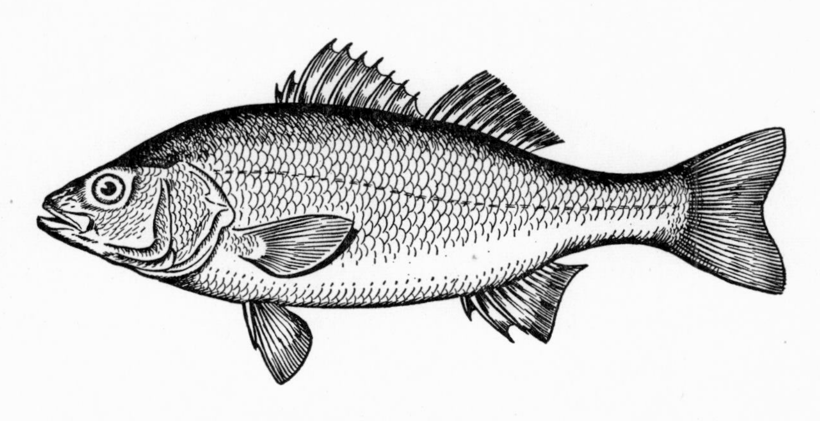

WHITE PERCH

Most white perch average from ½ to 1 pound in weight, although they often reach 2 or 3 pounds. The largest caught on rod and reel weighed 4 pounds, 12 ounces.

WHITE BASS

The white bass resembles the white perch in general appearance. However, the white bass has stripes running along its sides.

These fish are found mostly in the Great Lakes, the Mississippi River and its tributaries, and in the larger lakes and reservoirs of the Middle West.

White bass average from 1 to 2 pounds in weight and have been known to reach 4 or 5 pounds.

Almost any fresh-water fishing tackle, such as cane poles, bait-casting rods, spinning rods, and fly

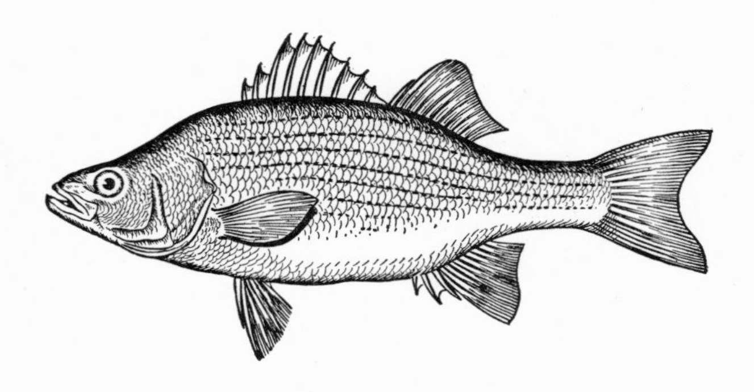

WHITE BASS

rods, can be used to catch pan fish. The most popular is the cane pole with a bobber and live bait; but for the most sport a fly rod is best.

The bait used for most pan fish is a small, lively garden worm. Small minnows are also good for such fish as crappies, yellow perch, and white bass. Grasshoppers, crickets, beetles, grubs, and meal worms will also catch pan fish.

Pan fish can also be caught on artificial lures such as small trout flies, tiny streamers, small spoons and spinners, and very small plugs. Small jigs can also be tried near the bottom.

Sunfish and crappies are usually found near shore around weed beds, lily pads, and sunken trees or logs. In rivers they prefer the quieter waters of pools. Yellow perch like deeper water, usually over sunken weeds. White bass are often found in the middle of a lake, chasing smaller bait fish or minnows.

Most pan fish travel in schools, and if you catch one you can be pretty sure there are more around. Yellow perch, white bass, and white perch often move about from one place to another. To locate them you often have to change spots. On some lakes you often see other rowboats anchored and fishing for pan fish, or there will be fishing from piers, docks, or from the shore if pan fish are biting. You can fish near them, but not so close as to interfere with their fishing.

Pan fish usually bite all day long, but during the hot summer months the early-morning or late-afternoon hours are best. Yellow perch, white perch, and white bass come close to shore, or head into streams and rivers entering lakes in the spring of the year. Here they lay eggs, or spawn. Fishing is often good during these spring runs if you can find the fish.

In fishing for pan fish, a cork or bobber should be used about 4 or 5 feet from the hook. When a fish first takes the bait, let him bite on it until he swallows it and starts moving away. When the float or bobber starts moving fast across the surface or sinks out of sight, lift the rod sharply to set the hook.

If you are using artificial lures such as flies, bugs,

spoons, or spinners do not reel or troll them too fast. Pan fish strike a slow-moving lure more readily than a fast-moving lure.

Pan fish are usually so plentiful in most waters that you are allowed to keep large catches. In some states and waters there is no limit, and you can keep all you can catch, so be sure that you know your state laws. It's quite a task cleaning and scaling the smaller pan fish; but after that you can look forward to delicious eating when the pan fish are fried golden brown.

The pike family

The members of the pike family are the muskellunge, the pike, and the pickerel. They all look alike in general body shape but vary in size and color.

MUSKELLUNGE

The muskellunge, or muskie, is our largest freshwater game fish. It has an olive-green back, gray sides, and dark spots and irregular stripes or bars over its body and fins. The muskellunge has a large mouth and jaws resembling an alligator. Most muskellunge run from 10 to 30 pounds in weight. The largest one ever caught weighed 69 pounds, 15 ounces.

Muskellunge are found in the St. Lawrence

MUSKELLUNGE

River, Great Lakes Basin and west through southern Canada to Minnesota, and also from northwestern Georgia and Tennessee to New York, Ohio, and Pennsylvania. They are found in these areas mostly in the larger lakes and rivers, where they stay near weed beds, sunken logs, or near lily pads.

Muskies can be caught on a large variety of lures, such as big surface and underwater plugs, large spoons, and spinners. They also take natural baits such as minnows, suckers, and other small fish. These should be fished live, and the muskie should be given plenty of time to swallow the bait. Trolling is a good way to take muskies, and big plugs and spoons are the best lures to use for this type of fishing. Whichever method you use, make sure that your rod is fairly stiff and that the line is stronger than that used for ordinary fresh-water fishing.

PIKE

The pike is smaller than the muskellunge, usually running from 5 to 20 pounds in weight. The largest caught on rod and reel weighed 46 pounds, 2 ounces. However, pike are more plentiful than muskellunge, especially in Canada. In the United States pike are found from New York through the Great Lakes to the upper Mississippi Valley. Although a pike looks something like a muskellunge in general body shape, it differs in coloring. A pike is usually a dark green or olive-gray, with many light-yellow bean-shaped spots all over its body. The belly is yellow-white.

PICKEREL

The pickerel is the smallest member of the pike family. This fish looks like a small pike or muskellunge, but it never grows bigger than 9 pounds, which is the largest one on record. Most pickerel caught are much smaller, usually running from 1 to 3 pounds.

The pickerel can be recognized by the "chain" markings found on its body. These are dark lines which look like links of a chain, overlaid on a background of greenish-yellow.

Pickerel are usually found in the shallower parts of a lake and quieter parts of a river, where they like to lie among the weeds and lily pads.

You can catch pickerel on small plugs, spoons,

spinners, and streamer flies. These can be cast or trolled behind a boat.

Another popular way to catch pickerel is with a long cane pole and a strip of pork rind on a hook. This is "skittered," or skipped, along the surface of the water near lily pads or other pickerel spots.

Pickerel are also caught with live minnows or frogs and a light float or bobber. When a pickerel grabs the bait let him run with it until he stops and swallows it.

Walleye

The walleye is sometimes called the walleyed pike, but it is actually a member of the perch family and is more closely related to the yellow perch than to the pike. The walleye has a large white eye which looks like glass. The body of this fish is dark olive green on the back, with yellow on the sides. Most of the walleyes caught weigh from 2 to 5 pounds. How-

WALLEYE

ever, they often reach more than 10 pounds and grow as big as 22 pounds.

The walleye is found in the eastern part of the United States and Canada, as far south as North Carolina, and also in the Great Lakes region and through the Mississippi Valley.

Walleyes prefer lakes and rivers with deep water, and gravel, sand, or rock bottoms. In rivers, look for them in the deeper pools and eddies. In lakes they frequent rock and gravel bars which drop off to deep water near by. They also gather in areas where rivers or streams enter a lake.

Although you can catch walleyes all day long in deeper waters by trolling or still-fishing, best results are usually obtained by fishing early in the morning and toward evening. Walleyes are very active at night, and come into shallow water after dark to feed. Fishing for walleyes is best early in the spring or late in the fall, when the water turns cold.

Walleyes can be caught on lures such as plugs, spoons, spinners, and streamer flies. They will also take natural baits such as minnows and lamprey eels.

Slow trolling is one of the best ways to catch walleyes. A popular lure is a June Bug spinner, with a minnow or several worms on the hook. Walleyes will also strike plugs and spoons which are reeled or

BULLHEAD

trolled deep and slow. In fact, any lures should be moved as slowly as possible.

Catfish

There are many kinds of catfish which can be caught in fresh-water rivers and lakes. Some, like the bullheads or horned pouts, are small, rarely reaching more than a few pounds in weight. Others, like the blue catfish, sometimes reach 150 pounds. Another large catfish is the flathead catfish, which may reach 100 pounds. One of the most popular catfish is the channel catfish, which grows to 50 pounds. The illustration above shows the bullhead, which is caught in many waters.

The larger catfish are found mostly in the Mississippi Valley region in the bigger rivers. Bullheads are found mostly east of the Rockies, and have also been introduced in the West, particularly in California.

Catfish are found in some lakes, but mostly in

the larger, sluggish rivers. They usually stay in the quiet, deep pools and eddies. Bullheads, like most catfish, bite best early in the morning, in the evening, and at night. The fishing is particularly good when the stream becomes muddy from recent rains.

Catfish are usually caught by still-fishing with hand lines, cane poles, or on rod and reel. They bite on many natural baits such as earthworms, minnows, pieces of fish, chunks of meat, and various "stink" baits made with combinations of cheese, ground meat, and flour. Even pieces of laundry soap on a hook have been used to catch catfish! For small catfish or bullheads use No. 1/0 or 2/0 hooks. For larger catfish, sizes 5/0, 6/0, or 7/0 are good. The Eagle Claw is a good hook for catfish.

Carp

Seventy-five years ago there were no carp in this country. Then they were sent from Europe and introduced into the eastern part of the United States. Now carp have become so plentiful in the lakes and rivers of many sections of the country that they are considered a pest.

The carp varies greatly in color, being yellowish, dark green, brown, or purplish-black, depending on the water where it is found. In general shape, the

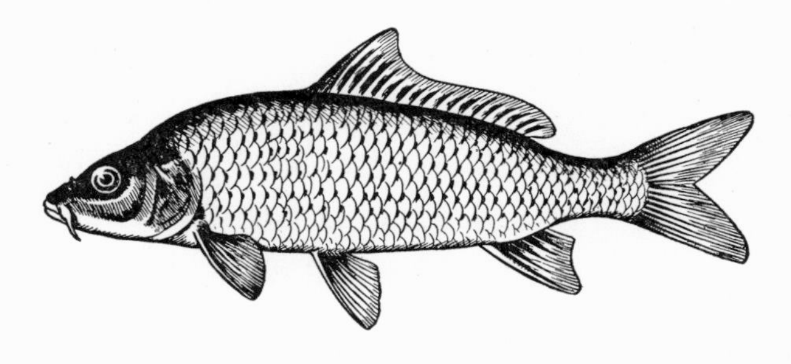

CARP

carp looks like the common goldfish, which is actually a small carp. The carp has round lips like the sucker.

Most of the carp caught will run from 2 to 8 pounds in weight. However, many carp weighing up to 15 or 20 pounds are caught, and they sometimes reach more than 50 pounds.

Carp can be found in many lakes, ponds, and rivers with mud bottoms and plenty of weeds or lily pads. In rivers they prefer the quieter pools and eddies. In lakes they often come close to shore to feed among the weeds. They can often be seen swimming near the surface or jumping out of the water with a loud splash.

Carp bite best during the late spring, summer, and early fall months. Fish for them early in the morning or in the evening and at night.

Carp can be caught on almost any kind of fishing

tackle: hand lines, bait-casting, spinning, and even light salt-water rods and reels. The best bait for carp is a dough ball made from flour and cornmeal with a little bit of sugar added. This is mixed with water and modeled into a pear-shaped mass around a hook. The best hook to use is an Eagle Claw in size 1 or 1/0 for small carp and 2/0 or 3/0 for big carp.

When fishing for carp make sure that the bait lies on the bottom. If you are fishing in a river with a strong current, you may have to use a sinker to keep the bait on the bottom. For best results cast the bait out so that it is at least 30 or 40 feet from shore. Then sit down and wait for a bite. Do not walk around or make any disturbance. Carp are very sensitive and suspicious fish. If they see you they will not bite.

When a carp first picks up the bait you will notice the line moving slightly. Do not pick up the line or rod at this time. Wait until you see the line moving out at a fast speed before you try to set the hook. Carp fight hard and will often give you several runs before they are brought to shore.

9 · Salt-Water Bottom-Fishing Tackle

Rods · Reels · Lines · Sinkers · Hooks · Rigs · How to bottom fish

Salt-water bottom fishing is popular with millions of anglers. You will see these people fishing from boats, piers, docks, bridges, and shore. This is not surprising. Bottom fishing requires such simple fishing tackle and bait that it doesn't cost much compared to other types of salt-water fishing. Bottom fishing is also easy—almost anyone can catch a good mess of fish when they are running. And, finally, most fish caught by bottom fishing make good eating.

Salt-water bottom fishing is similar to fresh-water still-fishing. In both types natural bait is used and is allowed to remain in the water at all times. The main difference is that in fresh water you often fish with a float to keep the bait off the bottom. In salt-

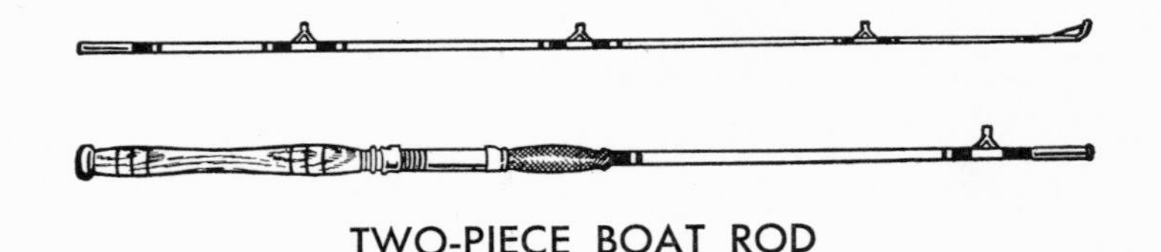

TWO-PIECE BOAT ROD

water bottom fishing, on the other hand, you keep the bait close to the bottom. You usually need heavy sinkers because of the deep water and strong tides.

Rods

The best rod for bottom fishing is the salt-water boat rod, which comes in one or two sections and runs from 5 to 6 feet in over-all length. Such a rod can be used from piers, bridges, boats, or shore. You can get either a solid glass or hollow glass boat rod for bottom fishing. These rods are ideal for boat fishing in deep water with heavy sinkers and for good-sized fish.

If you want to fish in shallow waters such as salt-water bays, inlets, and rivers, you can get a lighter boat rod, such as the weakfish or flounder rod. These rods are thinner, more limber, and usually shorter.

Some anglers also use salt-water spinning rods for bottom fishing. These are fine if you are catching small fish in shallow water and using light sinkers; but when fishing in deep waters, where heavy sinkers are needed, a boat rod is more suitable. (The drawing shows a salt-water boat rod.)

Reels

Almost any of the smaller salt-water reels can be used for bottom fishing, but the salt-water bay or boat reels are best for this purpose. The smaller reels can be used for shallow water, while the larger reels are better for deeper waters and big fish. The reel should have a free-spool lever with which to disengage the spool, and a star drag to adjust the tension.

Lines

You can use linen or braided nylon or Dacron lines for bottom fishing; but more and more people are using monofilament nylon lines for bottom fishing. These lines are strong, waterproof, and almost

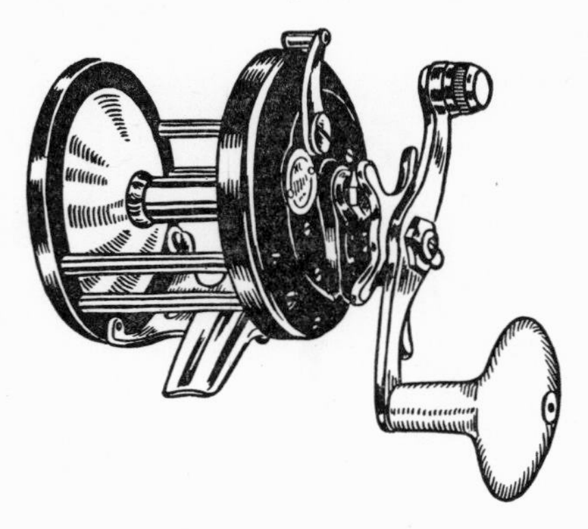

BOTTOM-FISHING REEL

invisible. Monofilament lines testing 20 or 25 pounds are used for shallow waters and small fish. For bigger fish in deeper waters and in rocky areas, mono lines testing 30, 40, or 50 pounds are best.

Sinkers

Sinkers are important in bottom fishing. They get the bait down to the bottom and hold it there despite the tide or current. Sinkers come in different sizes, shapes, and weights. Each is best suited for a particular kind of fishing and bottom.

The bank sinker is one of the most widely used, and is good for bottom fishing over rocks or sandy bottoms.

The diamond sinker is also popular, and is widely used from boats in deep water. The square sinker also works well in deep water.

The egg-shaped sinker, which has a hole run-

ning through the middle, is used for wary fish which nibble at the bait. The line runs through this sinker, and the angler can feel the lightest bite, but the fish cannot feel the weight of the sinker.

The round sinker is best when fishing over extremely rocky bottoms, where other types of sinkers get caught and are lost.

Different weights of sinkers should be carried at all times. If the water is shallow and the tide is weak, sinkers in the lighter weights of 2, 3, or 4 ounces can be used. For deeper water and stronger currents you may need sinkers weighing 6, 8, 10, or even 12 ounces.

Hooks

Hooks are also important in bottom fishing. Many types of hooks are used, depending on the fish to be caught and the bait used. One of the most popular hooks for salt-water bottom fishing is the Eagle Claw pattern. The O'Shaughnessy hook is another popular pattern for middling and large bottom fish. Other hooks often used are the Sproat, Carlisle, Pacific Bass, Virginia, and Chestertown. If you are not certain which hook to use for a certain fish, ask your local fishing tackle dealer to recommend the best type and size.

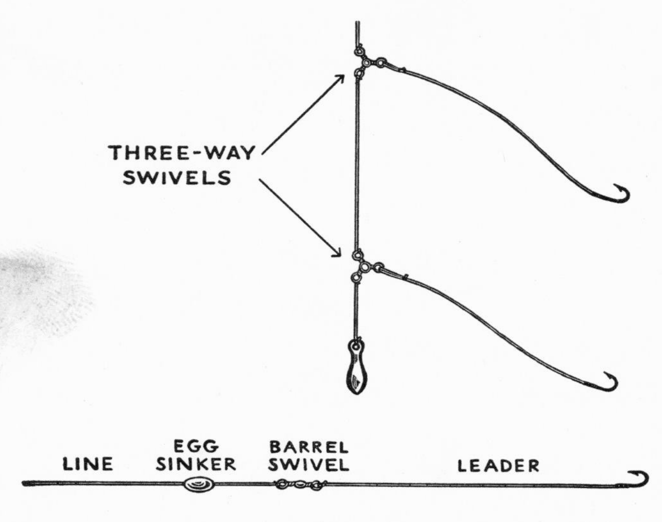

TWO BOTTOM-FISHING RIGS

Rigs

The basic bottom-fishing rig consists of a sinker tied to the end of the line with hooks tied above the sinker. One or two hooks are usually used, but as many as four or five can be used.

Another popular bottom-fishing rig makes use of an egg-shaped sinker. Here the hook is tied to one end of the nylon leader, while a barrel swivel is tied to the other end. Then the line is run through the hole in the egg-shaped sinker and is tied to the barrel swivel. The sinker slides up and down the fishing line. The drawing above shows these two bottom-fishing rigs.

You can make up such rigs by buying the eyed hooks, nylon leader material, swivels, and sinkers separately.

How to bottom fish

If you live near salt water you can find many spots where you can do bottom fishing. One of the best places for this is a pier or dock where you can go out and fish in deep water. Some of these piers are free to the public, while others are private and charge a small fee for fishing. Many piers have benches and shelters, and also sell or rent fishing tackle, bait, and soft drinks.

Most of the popular piers are crowded, and to get a good spot you have to come early in the morning. This is especially true when some kind of fish is running, and the news of the good catches spreads. However, most piers are fairly long and even the late-comers usually find a spot where they can squeeze in and fish.

Bridges are also good locations for bottom fishing, if fishing is allowed. If there is a sidewalk, fishing is usually safe; but on some bridges, where there is little room to stand, you have to watch out for moving autos and fishing can be dangerous. It doesn't pay to fish where there is danger of being hit by a car.

Bottom fishing is also done from the party or open boats which leave from many cities and towns. They are also called drift, or reef, boats in the South. Here you pay five or six dollars for a day's fishing. The boat takes you out into deep water, where you anchor or drift with the tide and wind. These boats usually supply the bait free. You have to bring your own rod, reel, and line. But they also rent fishing rods and reels, and sell hooks and sinkers on these boats. It's a good idea to take your lunch with you.

You can also bottom fish from a rowboat or skiff in many bays, sounds, and inlets. Such small boats can be rented in many places, with or without an outboard motor. In many places they will tow you out and bring you back from the fishing grounds. Boats can be rented anywhere from $1.50 to $5 a day without a motor, but if you want to try several spots in one day you need an outboard motor. With a motor it will cost a few dollars more, and you also have to buy your own bait. Most of the fishing stations which rent boats also sell bait.

You can also do bottom fishing from shore, jetties, or beaches. This is similar to surf fishing and will be covered in the next chapter.

Bottom fishing is a more sociable type of fishing than other kinds of salt-water angling. Bottom fishermen often gather in groups or fleets of boats in certain spots and fish near each other. That is one of the best ways to locate a good bottom-fishing spot. If you see many anglers or boats in one spot, it's a good idea to try there, too. In most cases they are catching fish, and you can join in the fun. Of course, you won't get so close that you interfere with the other anglers' fishing.

If you go on a party boat the captain will take you to the best fishing grounds, or if you rent a small boat the owner of the place will direct you to the most productive fishing spots.

Bottom fish usually gather where there is plenty of food for them. They eat worms, crabs, clams, mussels, oysters, and small fish. These are found around sunken wrecks, coral reefs, mussel and oyster beds, rocks, and seaweed.

If you are fishing from an anchored boat or from shore, cast or let the baited hook and sinker sink down to the bottom. The sinker should be heavy enough to stay on the bottom in the tide. When you get a bite, let the fish nibble a while until you feel a strong pull, then jerk hard with the rod tip to set the hook. Sometimes the fish bite better if you move the bait. To do this, lift the sinker from the bottom and then let it drop back again. Let the sinker lie on the bottom for a few seconds, and then lift it once again. Keep doing this regularly. If the tide is very strong you may have to let out a few feet of line each time you let the sinker drop back. If you don't feel bottom you may have to change to a heavier sinker.

You can also bottom fish by drifting in a boat, letting it move with the tide and wind. The sinker bounces along the bottom and you cover a lot of territory, at the same time moving the bait along the bottom to attract fish.

10 · Salt-Water Spinning Tackle

Rods · Reels · Lines · Accessories · How to spin cast

Salt-water spinning tackle has become very popular with people who fish from boats, piers, bridges, jetties, shore, and surf. Salt-water spinning tackle offers many advantages. The rods and reels are simple to operate, casting is easy, there are no backlashes, and no spooling of the line by hand. Spinning outfits are light and provide a lot of sport with even the smallest fish.

There are many salt-water spinning reels and rods to choose from. Because spinning tackle is expensive to buy, it is important to find out what kind of fishing you plan to do before choosing a salt-water spinning outfit.

Rods

Salt-water spinning rods come in three weights —light, medium, and heavy. The light rod can be a heavy fresh-water spinning rod, but for best results get one built for salt-water fishing. Such a rod can be cast with one hand, and should be from 6 to 7½ feet long. It should handle fishing lures weighing up to 1½ ounces. You can use such a rod from a boat or shore for casting light lures and catching smaller fish up to 20 pounds in weight.

The medium-weight rod will run from 7½ to 9 feet in over-all length. It will have a fairly long butt section so that it can be cast with two hands. It should be able to handle lures weighing up to 2 ounces and sinkers up to 3 or 4 ounces. You can use such a rod from boats, piers, bridges, shore, or surf for small, middling fish weighing up to 25 pounds. This is a good all-around salt-water spinning rod if you can afford to get only one outfit.

The heavy spinning rod is mostly a surf-fishing rod and will be between 9 and 11 feet long. It should handle lures up to 3 ounces and sinkers up to 4 or 5 ounces. With such a rod you can fish for the biggest fish found in the surf, such as striped bass and channel bass running up to 50 or 60 pounds.

SALT-WATER SPINNING REEL

Reels

Salt-water spinning reels are very similar to fresh-water spin reels except that they are larger and stronger, in order to be able to stand up in salt-water fishing and to hold more line of a heavier test. The metal parts of a salt-water spinning reel shouldn't corrode or rust. The bait and roller of such a reel should be made of a hard material and should operate efficiently. The reel should also have a smooth, dependable drag.

A good way to buy a salt-water spinning reel is to get an experienced fishing friend to advise you which reel to get. If he has used a certain spinning reel for several seasons, you can be pretty sure that the reel is sturdy and dependable.

Salt-water spinning reels come in two sizes, a small size which is suitable for use with a light- or medium-weight spinning rod, and a large size which is best when used with a heavy spinning rod.

Lines

Salt-water spinning lines are either braided nylon or Dacron or nylon monofilament. As with other types of fishing, most anglers prefer monofilament lines.

For the light salt-water spinning outfit, lines testing 8 to 10 pounds are best. For the medium-weight spinning outfit, lines testing 12 pounds can be used, while the heavier spinning outfits call for lines testing 15 or 20 pounds.

To take the shock of casting and wear and tear around rocks and sand, most salt-water anglers tie a heavier nylon leader to the end of their line. This should be at least 10 or 12 feet long and should test a few pounds more than the main fishing line on the reel.

You should also carry at least one extra spool filled with the same line you have on the reel, with slightly stronger line in case you need it.

Accessories

When fishing with spinning tackle in salt water you need a tackle box to keep your lures, sinkers, hooks, extra reel or line, and other equipment. For boat fishing a tackle box with compartments for fishing lures is best. But make sure that it is made for salt-water fishing, since the small boxes made for fresh-water fishing aren't large enough and they usually rust or corrode when they are wet or dampened with salt water.

If you fish from the surf a shoulder bag is better than a tackle box, since it leaves your hands free for carrying your other gear.

For surf fishing you also need boots or waders. These are discussed in more detail in the following chapter.

The artificial lures and natural baits used in salt-water spin fishing are also covered in Chapters 15 and 16.

How to spin cast

Casting with a light one-handed salt-water spinning rod is similar to casting with a fresh-water spinning rod.

When you use the longer, heavier spinning rods, two hands are necessary in casting. You go through the same motions as with a one-handed rod but you use two hands for more power and speed. The right hand grips the butt just above the reel, while the left hand holds the end of the butt. Then you bring the rod back over your head and stop it when it reaches a point slightly behind you. Now you immediately start the forward cast, snapping the rod sharply in front of you. To complete the cast you follow through and release the line from your forefinger, letting the lure shoot toward the target. To stop the cast you put the finger back on the reel spool or turn the handle.

11 · Surf-Fishing Tackle

Rods · Reels · Lines · Accessories · How to surf cast

Surf fishing offers some of the most exciting and satisfying fishing that can be done in salt water. There is something fascinating about casting into the breaking waves from the beach. Many people who have never caught fish from the surf find it hard to believe that big fish will come so close to shore. But every year quite a few striped bass and channel bass weighing 50 pounds or more are caught near the beach. Of course, surf fishing isn't easy, and you don't catch as many fish as in other forms of salt-water fishing. But most surf anglers would rather catch one fish from the surf than ten from a boat. When you cast into the ocean with a lure or bait you never know for sure what you will hook. It may be a small one-pound whiting or it may be a shark weighing more than 100 pounds. But no matter what you hook, you will get a good fight on the end of your line. Most fish found in the surf are powerful, and put up a satisfying fight.

Surf fishing is also one of the least expensive forms of salt-water fishing, once you buy the tackle. You do not have to rent or charter a boat. You do not have to fish from a special location, such as a pier or bridge. Instead, you have miles of beach or shore line where you can practice surf fishing, coming and going as you please. All this appeals to many anglers.

But to catch fish in the surf you must start off with the proper tackle. If you have a friend who does surf fishing, ask him to help you select the best outfit for the area you plan to fish. However, if you have no such friend, the following information will help you select the proper outfit.

Rods

Two types of outfits are used for surf fishing: salt-water spinning tackle and conventional surf tackle. Casting with a spinning reel is easier than with a conventional reel, so most surf anglers prefer a spinning rod and reel for their fishing. The spinning rod you need for surf fishing is the heavy rod, 9 to 11 feet long. This should have a fairly long handle or butt.

The conventional surf rod has smaller guides and is usually stiffer than a spinning rod. The best rod of this type to get is the medium-weight surf rod, which has a tip section from 6½ to 7½ feet in length. The butt, or handle, can be anywhere from 22 to 28 inches long. Such a rod should be able to cast lures up to 3 ounces and sinkers up to 6 ounces

Reels

If you have a spinning rod you will get a large, salt-water spinning reel to go with it. Such a reel is shown in the drawing on page 117.

If you buy a conventional surf rod you will need a conventional revolving-spool reel. These reels have light plastic or metal spools, a star drag, free

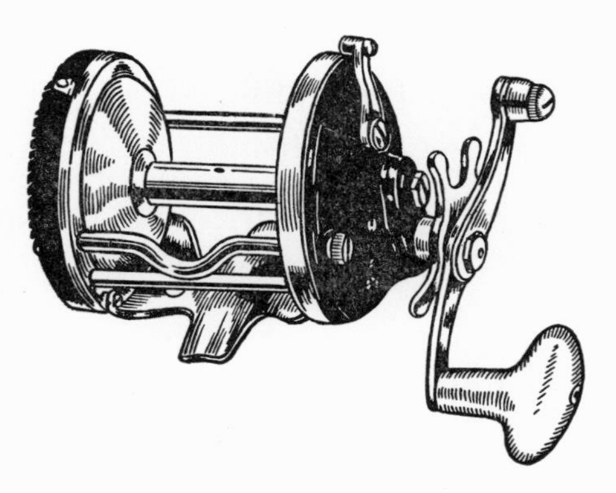

CONVENTIONAL SURF REEL

spool, and a fast gear ratio of at least 3 to 1. They come in different sizes, holding anywhere from 150 to 250 yards of 36-pound test line. The 150- or 200-yard surf reel is best for the medium-weight surf rod.

Lines

If you are using spinning tackle in the surf you will need nylon monofilament line testing anywhere from 12 to 20 pounds. The lighter lines are used with light lures and light spinning rods. The stronger lines are used with medium or heavy spin rods and heavy lures.

For conventional outfits you will need either nylon or Dacron braided surf-fishing line. Dacron lines are slightly thinner than nylon lines, which means that you can get a bit more line on your reel. Most surf anglers use lines testing 36 pounds with their conventional rods and reels. If the fish are running big or if you are fishing in rocky areas, you can use a 45-pound test line.

Accessories

The surf angler finds that he also needs a pair of boots or waders, especially when fishing in northern waters early in the spring or late in the fall. If you will be fishing mostly from sandy beaches or jetties, hip boots will be satisfactory. But for fishing in spots where you have to wade out into the water you will find waist-high waders better. Waders are also warmer if you fish in the fall.

You also need a waterproof jacket which can be worn over the waders. Such a jacket or parka has a hood, waterproof seams, and drawstring or snap around the neck and waist to keep the water out.

You will also want a canvas shoulder bag to carry lures, sinkers, hooks, extra line, or reel and other equipment if you plan to fish mostly in one spot all day. If, however, you plan to fish many spots or walk long distances along a beach, you will find a belt with small pouches for holding lures much better. The best type of belt for this is a surplus pistol belt, which is sold in many Army-Navy surplus stores. This belt has many holes to which you can attach small bags or pouches.

Surf anglers use a gaff, a big hook attached

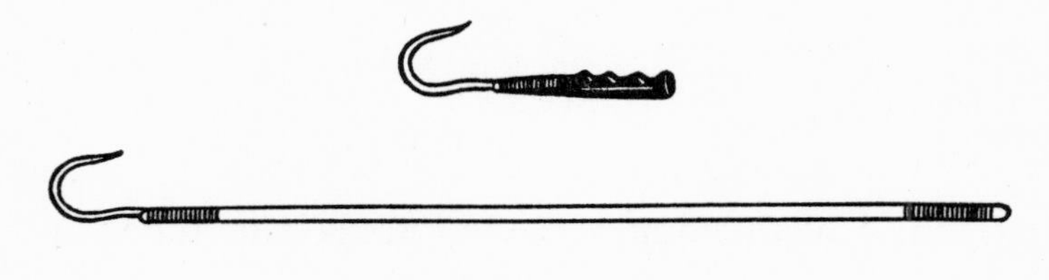

GAFFS

to a handle, for landing a fish when it is close to shore. For fishing from rock jetties you need a gaff with a handle at least 6 feet long or even more. If you are fishing from a beach you can use a gaff with a shorter handle. The illustration on page 125 shows these two types of gaffs.

For night fishing, surf anglers also need a flashlight or headlight of some sort. A headlight which can be worn around your neck or head is most convenient, since it leaves your hands free for casting or putting bait on the hook.

For fishing from sandy beaches with bait, a sand spike is needed. This is nothing more than a big, hollow metal tube with a pointed prong which is stuck into the sand. The rod butt is pushed into the hole to keep rod and reel away from the sand.

Other items often needed in surf fishing are a knife, sun glasses, can of oil for the reel, and, of course, extra sinkers and swivels.

How to surf cast

If you have a spinning outfit you can follow the instructions in Chapter 10.

When surf casting with a conventional rod and reel, stand with your feet well apart and face down the beach, with the water on your left. Your left foot is forward, pointing toward the ocean. Your right foot points down the beach. Now set the reel at free spool. Place your right thumb on the reel spool and grip the butt of the rod with your left hand. Start with the rod extending back over your right shoulder. Then, with a quick snap, bring the rod tip over your head. Pull down with your left hand and thrust the butt forward with your right hand. Twist your body to face the target. When the rod tip passes a point directly over your head, remove your thumb from the reel spool for a second. As the line starts to run off, put your thumb back on the spool. Keep it there at all times now. If the line runs off too fast apply a bit more pressure with your thumb. As the lure reaches the target and begins dropping, you stop the cast by pressing hard on the spool with your thumb.

To become a good surf caster with conventional tackle requires practice until you can feel the line moving out at the proper speed. Your thumb must act like a brake—applying pressure on the spool if it's going too fast and easing up if the spool slows down. After a while your timing and thumb pressure will become automatic, and casting will be easier. But in the beginning do not try to cast too far. It is important to cast smoothly and accurately.

12 · Offshore Fishing Tackle

This chapter covers offshore fishing, which is also called big-game and deep-sea fishing. In this fishing you go out in sports cruisers 26 to 40 feet long. These boats go offshore or out into the open ocean where they troll for big-game fish. These boats often fish for such monsters of the deep as swordfish, marlin, tuna, and sharks, some of which may weigh several hundred pounds. However, offshore boats also catch smaller game fish on many of their trips.

Offshore fishing costs less if three or four anglers get together and share the cost of a boat. In some places boats can be rented for half a day, but usually the charter boats go out for a full day.

If you charter a boat, the captain usually supplies the fishing tackle, so you don't have to buy a rod, reel, or line. This is a good thing, because not many people can afford to buy an offshore rod, reel, and line. Such tackle is expensive, and it is foolish to invest up to $150 or $200 for an offshore fishing outfit which you may use only once or twice a year.

Offshore rods are made of wood or glass and have strong guides, usually of the roller type. They have strong reel seats and thick butts or handles. The reels are large, with powerful drags and big spools which hold plenty of line. Lines used on offshore fish are made of either linen or Dacron and test anywhere from 30 to 180 pounds, depending on the size of the rod and reel and of the fish you expect to catch.

Long cable or single-strand wire leaders up to 15 feet long are used in offshore fishing. They come in various thicknesses and strengths from 27 to 480 pounds.

The sports cruisers equipped for offshore fishing have outriggers, which are two long poles on both sides of the boat. These can be spread out on both sides, and a line can be attached to each by means of a clothespin-like device. When a fish hits the bait or lure, the line jumps out of the clothespin and slackens, allowing the fish time to swallow the bait. Outriggers also keep the lines apart when they are trolled so that they don't tangle with each other and stay away from the wake of the boat.

Sports-fishing cruisers have a fishing chair, or fighting chair, in which you can sit when you fight a fish. These chairs have a foot rest and turn around so that you always face the fish.

They also have rod holders, metal tubes into which the rod is placed when you are not holding it.

For most offshore fishing you use whole fish or strips of fish for bait. They are rigged with one or two large hooks. These combinations are prepared in advance and kept frozen until used.

You can also use artificial lures such as feather or nylon jigs, spoons, and large wooden or plastic plugs when trolling offshore, especially for smaller fish.

When you go offshore fishing follow the advice of the captain, mate, or experienced fisherman. You may troll the bait in the water all day and get only one or two strikes from big fish. You must know what to do at this time or you will fail to hook the fish. If you follow instructions carefully, in most cases you will succeed.

The same thing holds true when you are fighting a big fish on the end of the line. Listen to what the captain or mate says and follow his advice. In fighting a big fish, the secret is not to let the fish rest but to keep him on the move as much as possible. When a fish is first hooked he should be allowed to run or jump. If the fish stops, you can start bringing him toward the boat. This is done by lowering the rod and reeling in line. Then lean back and raise the rod; then lower it again and reel in once more. Keep repeating this as long as the fish is not moving. When the fish starts running again, let him go and stop pumping. When he stops, you begin pumping once more. Do not touch the star drag on the reel unless you are told to do so. Usually when you get the fish near the boat you may have to tighten the drag a bit, but not too much, because if the fish starts running he may break the line or pull out the hook.

Offshore fishing can be uncomfortable if the water is rough. If you are bothered by seasickness, get some anti-nausea pills from your doctor. There are several kinds available.

It may take many trips before you are lucky enough to hook and land a big-game fish. However, once you do you will feel it was all worth while, and you will start fishing all over again for a still bigger fish or a different kind. There are always bigger fish offshore than have been caught so far.

13 · Salt-Water Baits

Sea worms · Clams · Squid · Menhaden · Silversides · Sand eel · Killifish · Mullet · Crabs · Shrimp

In salt-water fishing most anglers use natural baits to catch fish. From giant tuna to tiny porgies, most salt-water fish will take a properly presented natural bait. This means that the angler who knows most about natural salt-water baits, how they are caught, how they are hooked and rigged, and how they are presented will catch the most and biggest fish.

Some of these natural baits you can obtain yourself if you spend some time and energy. Other salt-water baits can be bought from coastal fishing tackle stores or bait dealers. The kind of bait you use will depend mostly on the fish you seek and the bait which is producing best at the time. It is always a good idea to find out which bait has been catching the most fish recently. It is also a good idea to take several kinds of bait on a fishing trip.

The following natural baits are the most popular.

Sea worms

Sea worms are effective bait for many salt-water fish. Two kinds of worms are generally used along the Atlantic Coast. One is the clam worm, often called the sandworm. It has a blue or green back, and pink or red undersides and "legs."

The other worm is the bloodworm, which is pink or flesh-colored, and has a smooth body tapering to a point on both ends. When touched or disturbed it shoots out a long head with four tiny, black jaws.

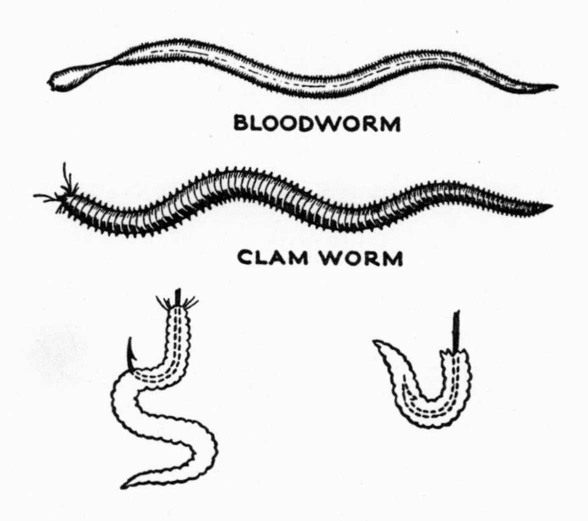

SEA WORMS AND METHODS OF HOOKING

Clam worms and bloodworms can be dug at low tide in many bays with mud flats. You can use a clam hoe or a garden fork to dig the worms from the mud. But it is hard work, so most anglers would rather buy the worms from a fishing tackle store.

When using worms for bait for big fish such as striped bass, use a whole worm or even two or three worms on a hook. For smaller fish such as flounders, porgies, and croakers, cut the worm into three or four pieces and use a small piece on the hook. (The drawing on page 133 shows how to put worms on a hook.)

Clams

There are many kinds of clams which can be used for bait. Some are big, like the surf or sea clam, often called the "skimmer" clam. This clam lives in the sand along the beaches of the Atlantic Coast. After a storm or heavy sea these clams are often washed up on the beach and can be picked up at low

CLAM AND METHOD OF HOOKING

tide. You can also buy these clams from fishing tackle stores and bait dealers located near the ocean.

Another clam which can be used for bait is the hard clam, which is found in bays. These clams are smaller and are usually sold in restaurants and fish markets. You can also obtain them by feeling for them in shallow water with your bare feet, or by raking them out with a clam hoe.

The soft meaty part of the clam is used for bait. You can open clams by inserting a knife between the shells or by cracking them against a rock or other hard surface. The meat inside can be cut up into small sections for small fish, or you can use the entire insides of a clam for big fish. Run the hook through the clam meat two or three times so that it will stay on the hook. (The illustration shows a clam and how to put the meat on a hook.)

Squid

The squid is a relative of the octopus which is widely used for fish bait. Squid bait is tough, white, and stays on a hook for a long time. Most of all, salt-water fish like it. Sometimes squid are washed ashore and can be picked up at low tide, but usually they are bought from tackle stores, bait dealers, or fish markets. Nowadays they are frozen in one-pound

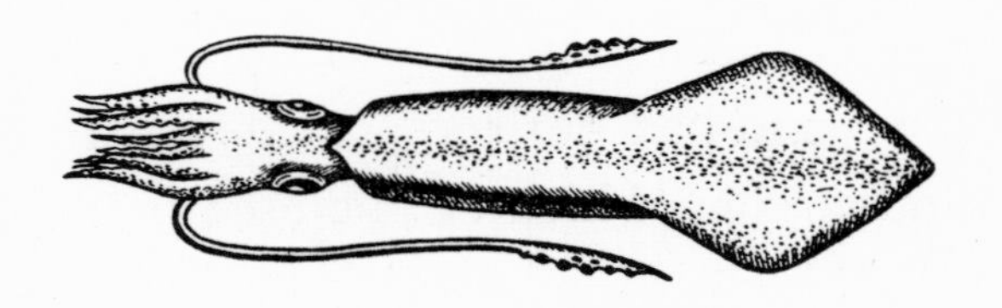

SQUID AND METHOD OF HOOKING

packages and sold for bait. If you buy the squid fresh they should be kept on ice until used.

Squid are cleaned by removing the insides and the thin skin around the body. Then they are cut into strips or small pieces. For big fish such as striped bass, a whole squid or the head is often used for bait.

Menhaden

The menhaden, or mossbunker, is a fish which is often used for bait and chum, which is bits of bait spread on the water to attract fish. Called "bunker" for short, this fish is very oily and is ground up and thrown into the water to attract larger fish. The oil and pieces of menhaden spread out and create a "slick" which draws fish near the boat. This is done for bluefish, tuna, bonito, albacore, sharks, and many other salt-water fish.

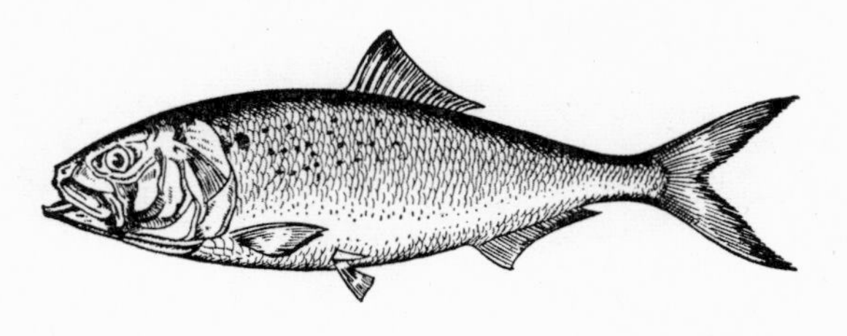

MENHADEN

The menhaden also makes good bait if it is cut into chunks and placed on a hook. It can be used for striped bass, bluefish, weakfish, channel bass, and other fish.

Silversides

The silversides, also called a spearing, is another bait fish used in salt-water fishing. It is found close to shore in the surf, in bays, inlets, and salt-water creeks. You can catch silversides with a seine or other net, but most fishermen buy them in a fishing tackle store or fish market. They are used on a hook to catch silver hake, bluefish, weakfish, mackerel, fluke, and others.

Sand eel

The sand eel, or sand launce, is another generally small, useful bait fish. It is a long, slim fish which looks like a tiny eel. Sand eels are sometimes

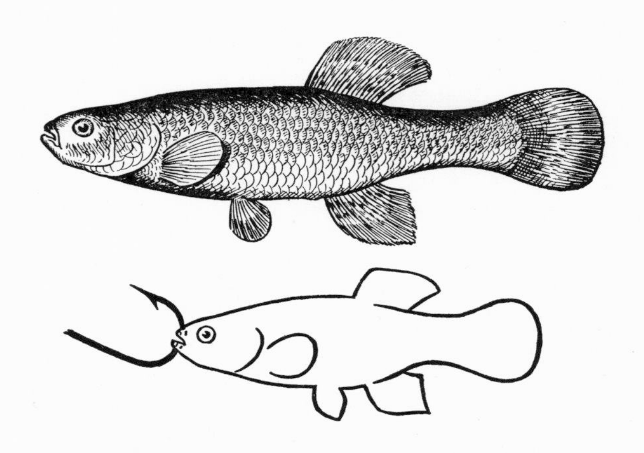

KILLIFISH AND METHOD OF HOOKING

sold in fishing tackle stores or at bait dealers. They make good bait for silver hake, bluefish, striped bass, fluke, and other fish. Hook a sand eel through the eye and then in the middle of the body.

Killifish

The killifish, or mummichog, often called "killie" for short, is a popular bait for fluke or summer flounders. It is sold alive at fishing tackle stores and bait dealers. You can catch your own killies in a minnow trap baited with crushed crabs, clams, or mussels. Killies live a long time if they are hooked through the lips as shown in the illustration. Killies are kept alive in small boxes or cages submerged in the water. Besides fluke you can catch small bluefish, sea bass, and weakfish with killies.

Mullet

The mullet is another widely used bait fish. Mullet are found swimming close to shore in large schools. Here they are caught in long seines. Mullet are also sold by bait dealers, fishing tackle stores, and in fish markets. The large mullet are cut up into chunks or strips before being placed on a hook, while the smaller mullet can be used whole. Mullet will catch striped bass, bluefish, channel bass, weakfish, tarpon, snappers, and many other salt-water fish.

Crabs

There are many kinds of crabs that can be used for bait. Three of the most commonly used are the

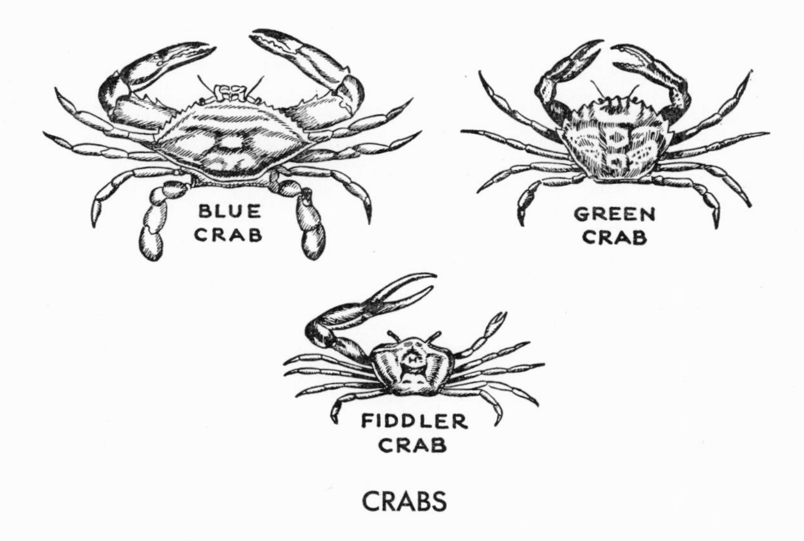

CRABS

blue crab, the green crab, and the fiddler crab. The blue crab is the big crab often sold in restaurants and fish markets. For bait the best blue crabs are not the hard ones. You should try to get the shedder or soft-shell crabs. A shedder crab has a hard shell, but if you break it the newly formed soft shell is underneath. A soft-shell crab already has thrown off its hard shell and is waiting for the new one to get hard. Both of these stages of the blue crab make good bait. You can sometimes catch the blue crabs with a long-handled crab net in shallow water in bays. You can use a whole crab for big fish such as striped bass or channel bass. Smaller pieces are used for weakfish, bluefish, whiting, and other fish. You may have to tie the crab around the hook with fine sewing thread to keep it from falling off the hook.

The green crab, found around rocks and jetties, is used for blackfish, or tautog. You can find this crab by turning over the smaller rocks at low tide. The larger green crabs are cut in half or quartered, while the smaller ones are used whole.

Fiddler crabs are found in holes in bay marshes that have mud and sandy bottoms. Two kinds are commonly used for bait: the dark-green "mud fiddler" and the tan-colored or lighter "china-back" fiddler. You can catch fiddlers at low tide by scoop-

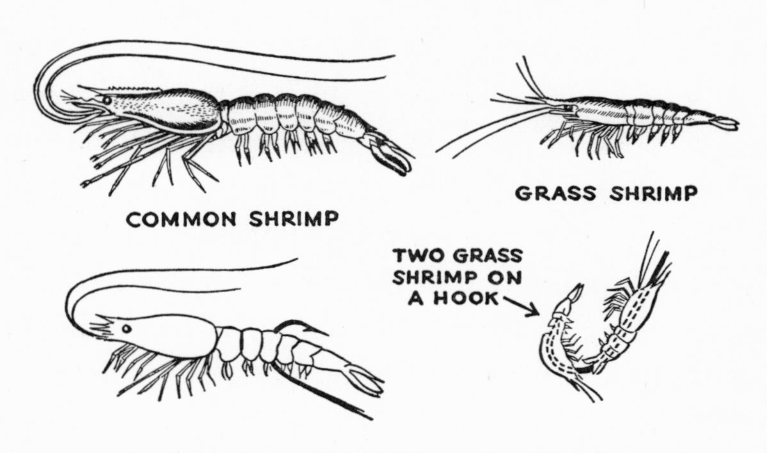

SHRIMP AND METHODS OF HOOKING

ing them up with a net or by hand. They are also sold in fishing tackle stores.

Shrimp

In Florida and other southern waters, live shrimp are used for bait to catch many kinds of fish. These shrimp are sold by fishing tackle stores and bait dealers and are kept in a container filled with salt water until used. They are hooked through the tail or back for best results. You can also use dead shrimp which have been frozen or kept on ice. Shrimp will catch sea trout, channel bass, or redfish, snappers, snook, and many other fish in southern waters.

In northern waters a smaller variety of shrimp

known as the grass shrimp or common prawn is used for chum and bait. These small shrimp are used mainly for weakfish, which are attracted to the boat by chumming. Here you throw three or four of the shrimp into the water at regular intervals. Then you can bait a hook with the same shrimp by placing two, three, or four of them on one hook. Besides weakfish, the grass shrimp will also attract striped bass, blackfish, flounders, porgies, and other salt-water fish when used as chum. (The illustration on page 141 shows the two kinds of shrimp and how they are hooked.)

This covers most of the important baits used in salt-water fishing. There are many others which can be found or bought and used at times. In fact, almost any small worm, shellfish, or bait fish can be tried as bait.

14 · Salt-Water Lures

Spoons · Spinners · Plugs ·
Metal squids · Jigs · Eel lures

Many of the lures which are used in fresh-water fishing can also be used for salt-water fishing. However, as a general rule, salt-water lures are heavier, stronger, and larger than fresh-water types. The following lures are used in salt-water fishing.

Spoons

There are many sizes, shapes, and weights of spoons used for salt-water fishing. They come in brass, copper, nickel, chrome, and painted finishes. The most popular finish for salt-water fishing is a nickel- or chrome-plated spoon. Salt-water spoons run from the small 2-inch size up to large 12-inch spoons. These big spoons, often called bunker spoons,

SALT-WATER SPINNER

are used when trolling for big striped bass, bluefish, and other large salt-water fish. Although some of the smaller spoons may be equipped with treble hooks, most salt-water spoons have a strong single hook attached.

Spinners

Spinners aren't used as often in salt-water fishing as in fresh water, and when they are used there is generally some kind of bait as well. The most popular type of salt-water spinner is the Cape Cod spinner, which has blades shaped like a willow leaf. This spinner is trolled slowly for striped bass in bays and inlets. Two or more bloodworms are usually placed on the hook behind the spinner. Other spinners used in salt-water fishing are the fluke and snapper spinners, which have two blades and a single hook. A small bait fish is usually put on the hook.

Plugs

Wooden and plastic plugs have recently become very popular in salt-water fishing. There are many

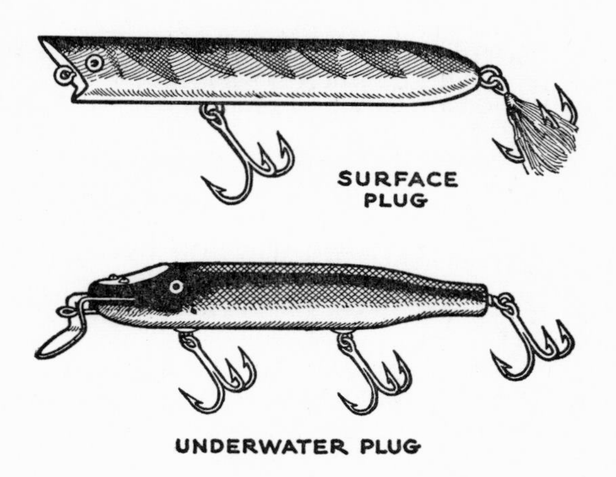

SALT-WATER PLUGS

types of plugs of different sizes, shapes, weights, and actions. The plugs can be divided into two groups: surface and underwater types. The surface plugs include poppers, flap-tails, and swimmers. These are reeled in on top of the water and create a disturbance or splash which makes them look like crippled bait fish. They imitate such small fish as menhaden, mullet, herring, and silversides.

Underwater plugs used in salt water have metal lips or shapes which cause them to dive and dart or wriggle under the water. The color of the plug used is not too important in surface types, but should be considered in underwater models. The underwater plugs having a blue mullet or a silver finish are good for most salt-water fish.

Both surface and underwater plugs for salt-water fishing come in various sizes, from small 3-inch lengths up to 12 inches. The small plugs are good for small fish and light tackle, while the heavier models are used for large fish and heavy tackle.

Metal squids

Metal squids have been used to catch fish in the surf for many years. They can also be used for casting or trolling from a boat. Metal squids come in different shapes, sizes, and weights; some are short and broad, others are long and slim. They all imitate some small fish found in salt water. The best metal squids are molded from block tin with only a little lead added; others are chrome-plated or painted; some squids have bucktail hair or feathers wound around the hook. Some squids have a hook molded right into the body of the lure. Others have a free-swinging hook. Squids can be used plain or they can have a piece of pork rind attached to the hook. Most metal squids weigh from 1 to 3 ounces.

Jigs

Jigs are also called bucktails, bugeyes, bullheads, and barracudas. They come in different weights, colors, and sizes. Jigs have heavy heads made from

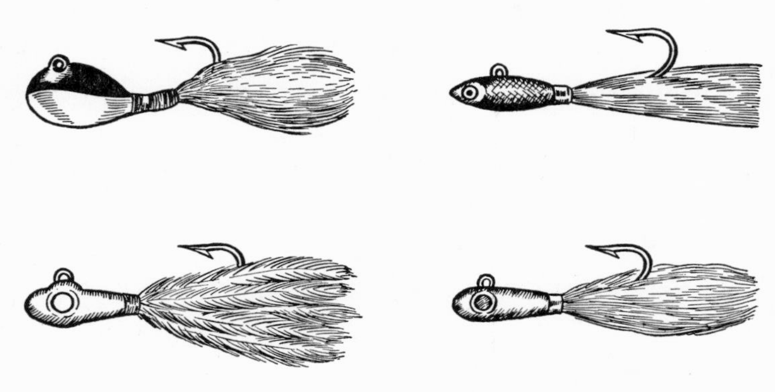

JIGS

lead or other metal, and have skirts of feathers, hair, nylon, or plastic wrapped around the hook. The metal head can be chrome-plated, or painted in any color. Most jigs used in salt-water fishing have silver, white, or yellow heads, and white or yellow skirts of bucktail or feathers.

The smaller, lighter jigs with small hooks are used with light fishing tackle. The larger, heavier jigs with big hooks are used with heavy fishing tackle and for trolling. Jigs can be cast or trolled behind a boat to catch many salt-water fish. They can also be bounced up and down on the bottom to catch many fish which are usually caught on natural baits.

Eel lures

Small live eels are often rigged with two or more hooks and are used to catch such fish as striped bass and bluefish. These eels can be anywhere from 10 to 18 inches long, and are often caught in eel pots by the anglers themselves. But they can also be bought all ready to use in jars in most fishing tackle stores. The eels can be cast or trolled, but are mostly used in the surf at night when fishing for striped bass.

Lures are also made from eelskins alone. Here the skin is turned inside out and tied around a weighted head similar to a jig. There is usually a ring or groove around which the skin can be tied. A hole in the metal head permits water to enter to inflate the skin when it is being reeled or trolled. Eelskin lures are used mostly for striped bass and bluefish.

15 · Making Salt-Water Lures

Making salt-water plugs · Making metal squids · Making jigs

As was the case with fresh-water lures, many of the salt-water lures described in the previous chapter can be made at home. You not only save money but also have a delightful hobby during the winter when fishing is slow. The fishing lures you make in advance will replace those you will lose during the coming fishing season.

When making spinners and spoons for salt-water fishing you can follow most of the instructions in Chapter 7 for making fresh-water lures. The only difference is that in making salt-water spinners and spoons you usually use larger and stronger hooks, heavier wire, and larger spinner blades and spoons.

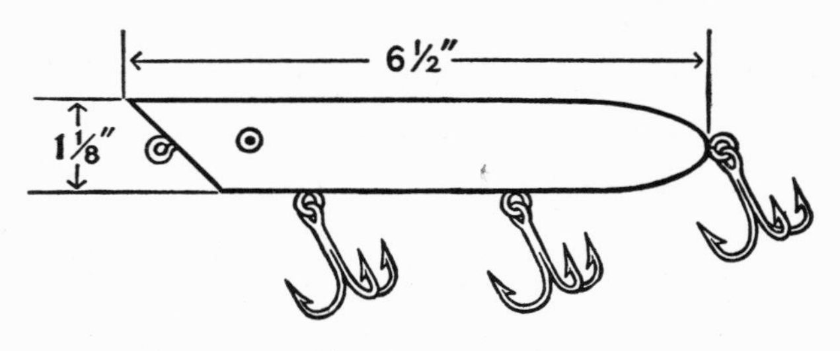

SURFACE POPPER

Making salt-water plugs

You can also follow the instructions for making fresh-water plugs in Chapter 7 when making salt-water types. While plugs used in salt water require stronger hooks and longer, heavier screw eyes, fresh-water plugs are just right in size for casting with a light salt-water spinning outfit.

If, however, you plan to use the plugs for surf fishing with heavy tackle, you will have to make them larger and heavier. These can be twice as long and as thick as those used for fresh-water fishing.

One plug which can be made for salt-water fishing is the surface popper shown in the illustration above. This plug should be about 6½ inches long and about 1⅛ inches thick. The head is cut at a 45-degree angle as shown. It should have three No. 5/0 treble hooks attached. Try to get extra-strong treble hooks when you make this plug. Many salt-water fish are big and powerful, and will straighten out ordinary thin-wire treble hooks. The same is true of the screw eyes you use on salt-water plugs. Try to get large, heavy-wire screw eyes made from brass. You can use iron screw eyes, but these eventually rust away.

Cedar wood can be used to make salt-water plugs, although it is light in weight. To make heavier plugs, which are easier to cast, you can use birch, fir, maple, or walnut.

To form a plug use a saw, rasp, and coarse file to shape the body. Then take a smooth file and sandpaper to finish it. Of course, if you are lucky enough to have a lathe at home, you can shape the plugs much faster. However, it is surprising how quickly you can turn out the plugs with ordinary hand tools after you have made a few of them.

Making metal squids

Anglers who use metal squids for surf casting or trolling from a boat can make up their own lures inexpensively from a plaster cast. You can copy an

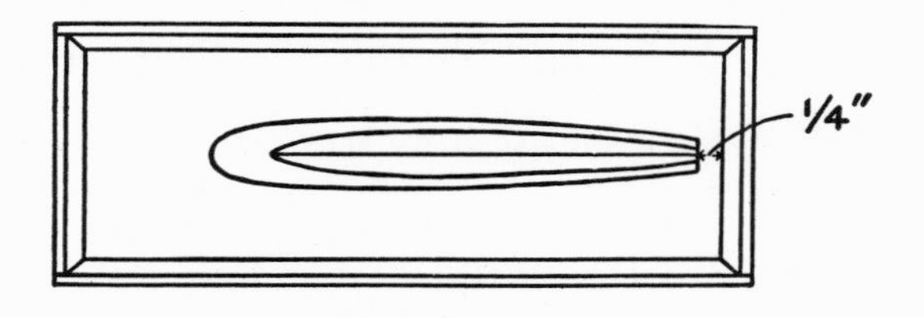

METAL SQUID PATTERN IN BOX

existing model of metal squid by cutting or filing off the hook and removing the eyelet. Then the squid should be smoothed with fine steel wool, and the hole where the eyelet was should be filled with clay.

You can also carve an original squid from some soft wood like balsa and make a cast from this. Before you use this wooden pattern, however, first paint or varnish it so it doesn't absorb water from the wet plaster.

Now take the model or pattern of the squid you are going to cast and give it a coat of vaseline to prevent the plaster from adhering to it. Get a small cardboard box about 5 or 6 inches long, 2 inches wide, and about 1½ inches deep. The boxes used to hold fishing plugs are good. Smear the inside of this box with vaseline also. Now place the model of the squid in the center of this box with the flat side down. The tail end of the squid (which held the hook) should be only about a quarter of an inch from one end of the box. (See drawing on page 151.)

Your next step is to mix some plaster of Paris in a small pot. You can buy this plaster in any hardware or paint store, and mix it with water. As you sift the plaster into the water, feel around with your hands to break up any lumps. When the plaster is thick but can still be poured, spill some into the box containing the metal squid. Fill the box almost to the top, leaving the flat top of the metal squid exposed. Then wait about 20 or 30 minutes for the plaster to harden.

Now cut open the box carefully and remove the plaster cast. With the point of a knife loosen the squid model and take it out without damaging the plaster cast. It will take at least one week for the plaster cast to dry. Then you can carve a pouring hole at the head of the cast and a slot to take the hook on the opposite end. You also need a metal plate, such as brass or copper ⅛ of an inch thick, for a cover for the plaster mold.

The cast should be thoroughly dry before you use it, or else hot metal will spatter in all directions when poured. To use the plaster mold all you have to do is fit a hook into the slot and place the metal cover over it.

Now melt some block tin mixed with a small amount of lead, and pour it into the mold. Hold the plaster cast and cover together, and pour the hot metal through the pouring hole. You can use a C-clamp to hold the mold and metal cover together if you want. After pouring, wait at least a minute before you separate the mold.

When working with hot metal it is, of course,

extremely important to be careful about getting burned or ruining your kitchen. Whenever possible this sort of work should be done outdoors or in a basement workshop.

The metal squids will need some finishing when they come out of the mold. They have to be trimmed, filed, and a hole must be drilled for an eyelet at the head of the lure. Feathers or bucktail are usually wrapped around the hook. The plaster mold is usually good for about a dozen or two dozen squids before it breaks up and becomes unusable.

You can also buy complete metal molds from E. L. Sweet & Son, 2407 Niagara Falls Blvd., Tonawanda, New York. Such molds will last for years and will turn out thousands of metal squids.

Making jigs

Jigs are effective in both fresh- and salt-water fishing. They are usually fished deep, near the bottom, where they get hung up and lost. By making your own jigs you can always have plenty on hand.

You can easily make a plaster mold to pour these lures in large numbers. The first step in making one is to get a pattern or model to copy. You can buy a jig in a fishing tackle store for this, or you can carve out a pattern from soft wood.

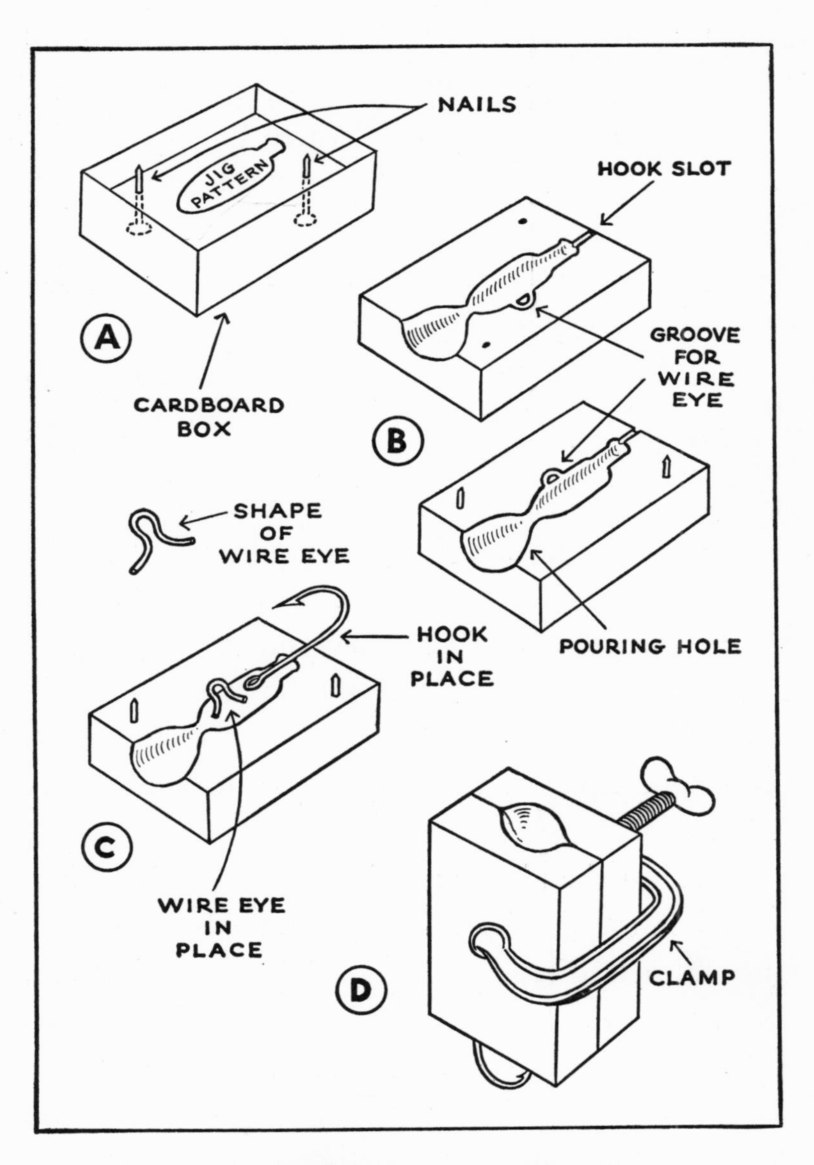

MAKING PLASTER MOLD FOR JIGS

The next step is to get a small cardboard box and pour in enough plaster of Paris to fill it halfway. Then you smear the jig pattern to be copied with vaseline, and press it halfway into the wet plaster. Then take two nails and sink them into the wet plaster, as shown in *A*. These nails will act as locating pins when you pour the jigs.

After the first half of the plaster mold hardens, brush the entire surface with heavy oil. Then mix more plaster of Paris and pour it into the box to the top. When this plaster gets hard, break up the cardboard box and separate the two halves, using a knife blade. Then set the two plaster casts aside to dry for several days. After they are dry you carve out pouring holes and a slot to take the hook, as shown in *B*. You can also cut out a groove to take a wire eyelet. You can form such a wire eye from brass or copper wire.

When the plaster cast is completely dry, place a hook in the slot (*C*). Then get some lead or block tin and melt it in a ladle over a gas or electric stove. Now you are ready to put the two plaster casts together and pour your jigs (*D*). When you do this be very careful not to spill any hot lead or tin on yourself, and make sure that the plaster cast is thoroughly dry, or else the hot lead will shoot out and spatter all over. It usually takes from one to two weeks for the plaster casts to dry thoroughly.

Instead of making a plaster mold for jigs you can also buy a finished metal mold very cheaply. These can be ordered from Herter's Inc., Waseca, Minnesota, or from Netcraft Co., 3101 Sylvania Ave., Toledo, Ohio. Such a metal mold will last forever and will make thousands of jigs.

After the jigs have been poured they require some trimming with cutting pliers and a file. Then you can tie on some bucktail or feathers around the hook to finish the lure. You can also paint the metal head in any color you like.

Of course, the lures above aren't the only ones you can make yourself; almost any fishing lure you see can be copied at home. It may not look as perfect as a store-bought lure, but it will catch fish and, after all, that's all that counts.

16 · Salt-Water Fish

Bottom fish · Surf fish · Game fish

Bottom fish

There are many kinds of fish which can be caught by bottom fishing in salt water. You not only can catch bottom fish but also many so-called "game fish" which usually swim near the surface. The following are some of the more popular fishes taken by bottom fishing.

FLOUNDERS

There are many kinds of flounders caught in the ocean, but the winter flounder found along the Atlantic Coast is the most numerous. It is found from Canada to North Carolina but is most plentiful from Massachusetts to New Jersey. Flounders average

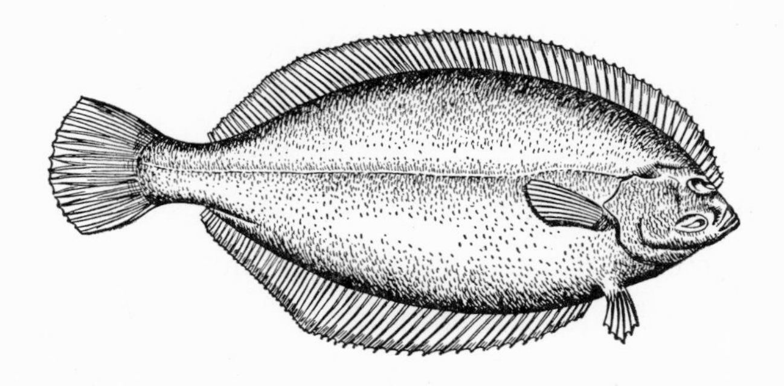

WINTER FLOUNDER

about one pound in weight but can reach 5 or 6 pounds. These fish like mud or sand bottoms in bays, inlets, and channels.

To catch them you use Chestertown or Eagle Claw flounder hooks in sizes 7 or 9 baited with pieces of bloodworm, sandworm, clam, or mussel.

The best months for flounder fishing are March, April, May, October, and November.

Another popular flounder is the summer flounder, also known as the fluke. The fluke has a larger mouth than the winter flounder and grows much bigger, sometimes reaching 20 pounds. Most of the fluke caught, however, run from 1 to 5 pounds. They are found along most of the Atlantic Coast, but are most numerous from Massachusetts to New Jersey. Fluke fishing is best in the bays, channels, inlets, and up to a mile or two off the beaches in the ocean. Here the boats drift with the tide or wind and let the sinker and bait bounce along the bottom. The biggest fluke are usually caught around sunken wrecks or rocks.

For fluke you use long-shanked hooks, such as the Carlisle, in sizes 3/0, 4/0, 5/0, or 6/0, depending on the size of the fish running. These are tied on a long 3-foot leader a few inches above the sinker. The best bait for fluke is a live killifish or some other small bait fish such as a spearing or sand eel. These are usually used with a strip of squid bait on the hook first. Then the small fish is added. Sometimes a spinner or two are added above the bait. The best months for fluke are June, July, August, and September.

BLACKFISH

The blackfish, or tautog, is another popular bottom fish caught from Canada to New Jersey. This is a dark, thick fish, with big buckteeth and round lips, usually running from 1 to 5 pounds in weight, but occasionally reaching 20 pounds.

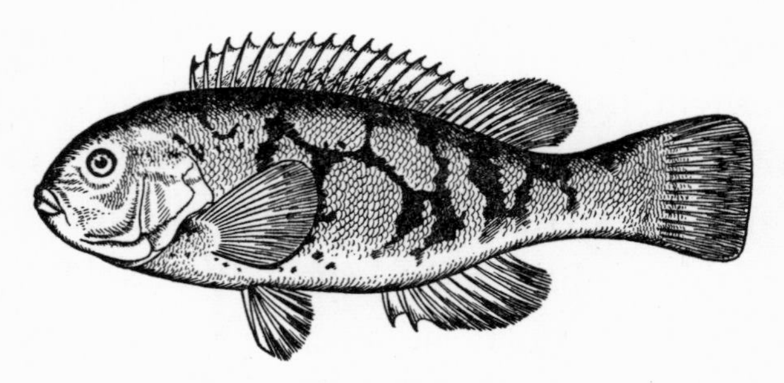

BLACKFISH

Blackfish are found over rocky bottoms, oyster and mussel beds, and around sunken wrecks. They also feed around jetties or breakwaters. You lose a lot of sinkers and hooks when blackfishing but this can't be avoided if you want to catch them.

To catch these fish you need a fairly stiff, strong boat rod and Virginia hooks in sizes 2 to 7, depending on the size of the fish. You can also use Eagle Claw hooks in sizes 1/0 and 3/0. One or two hooks should be tied low, just above the sinker. For bait you can use a piece of clam, sandworm, or a fiddler crab. Green crabs can also be used if you can get them. Give a blackfish plenty of time to swallow the bait before you set the hook.

SEA BASS

The sea bass is another bottom fish found and caught along the Atlantic Coast from Massachusetts to North Carolina. This fish is dark in color, almost

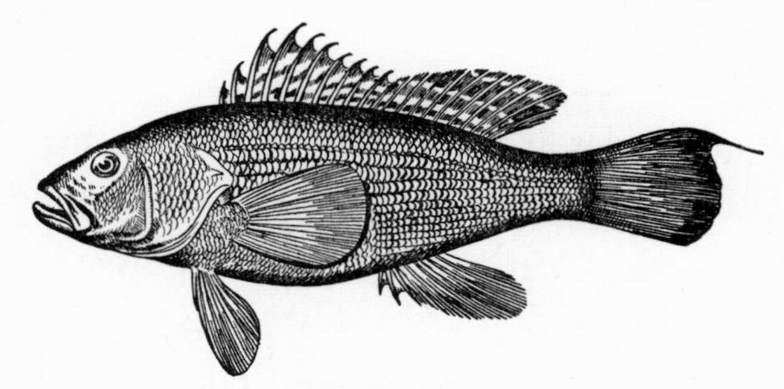

SEA BASS

black, and has a big head and mouth. Most sea bass will run from 1 to 3 pounds in weight. The larger ones are called humpbacks because of the shape of their backs. These are also darker and bluish in color. Sea bass sometimes reach 8 pounds in weight, and they make good eating.

The smaller sea bass are found in bays, inlets, and close to shore in the ocean. The larger ones are found in deeper water around wrecks or over mussel beds. They also like rocky bottoms, where they can feed on crabs and small fishes.

You can use Eagle Claw hooks in sizes 2/0 or 3/0 for small sea bass and 4/0 or 5/0 for larger ones. The hooks can be baited with a large piece of clam, squid, or fish. Sea bass are very greedy and bite quickly as soon as the bait reaches the bottom. They will steal the bait from a hook in a short time, so it pays to reel in after every bite to see if the hooks are still covered with bait.

PORGIES

The porgies are real "pan fish of the sea," and, like sunfish in fresh water, they are the most numerous of bottom fish. The northern porgy is found from Massachusetts to the Carolinas, while other porgies are found in southern waters. The northern

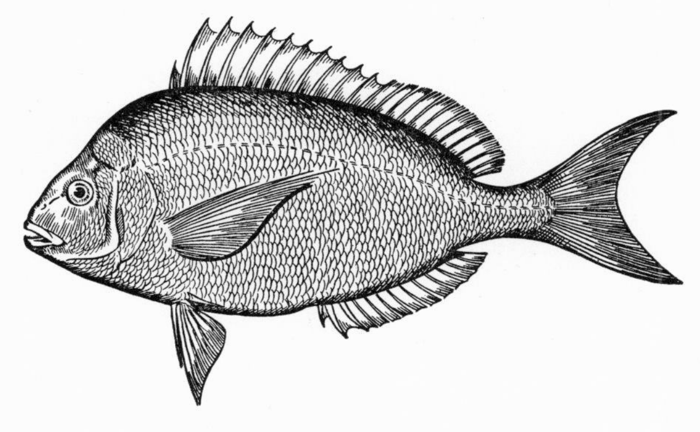

PORGY

porgy, also called the scup, is a deep-bodied fish with large fins and sharp spines. Porgies average about 1 pound in weight and grow to 3 or 4 pounds.

When porgies arrive in the spring, around May and June, they come in big schools numbering thousands if not millions of fish. The smaller porgies are caught in bays and inlets near shore, while the larger ones stay in deeper water offshore. They are most numerous around mussel or oyster beds and over rocky bottoms. A line baited with three hooks will often catch them two or three at a time.

They are usually caught on No. 1/0 or 2/0 hooks such as the Eagle Claw, baited with pieces of clam. They will also bite on worms, squid, and shrimp.

They put up a good fight on light tackle, so it's best to use a limber rod for them.

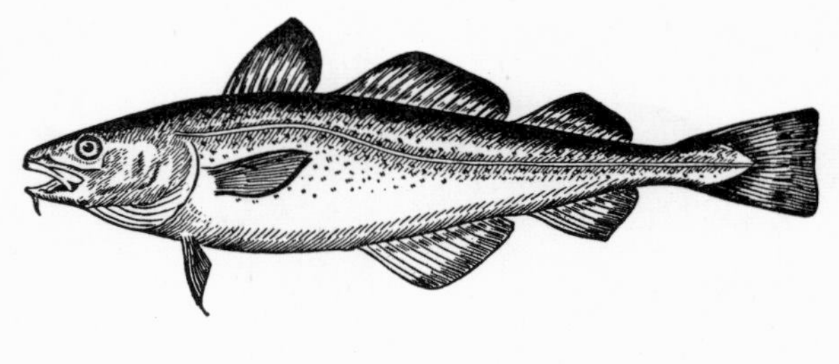

COD

COD

During the winter months from November to March, the most popular bottom fish caught in the North Atlantic is the codfish. This is a big fish, usually weighing from 3 to 20 pounds, but often running up to 30 pounds or more in weight. The largest caught on rod and reel weighed 74 pounds, and cod can grow well over 100 pounds.

Codfishing is generally done from an anchored or drifting boat, over rocky or mussel bottoms and around offshore banks, or shallower spots. Sometimes they come close to shore, where they can be caught from piers or jetties.

You need a strong boat rod for codfish because you often use sinkers weighing 10 or 12 ounces and large baits. Big 7/0 or 8/0 Eagle Claw or Sproat hooks are baited with large pieces of clam or fish for codfish.

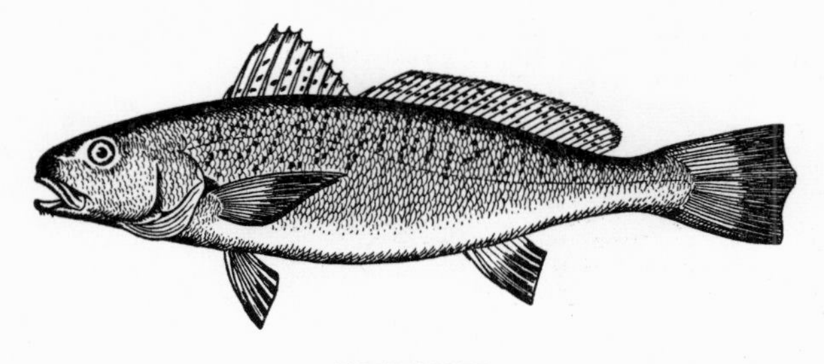

CROAKER

CROAKER

The croaker is a small bottom fish which is very plentiful from Maryland south to the Gulf of Mexico. It is brassy in color and has dark spots on the back and upper fins. This fish gets its name from the croaking sound it makes. The croaker averages about a pound in weight but sometimes reaches 5 pounds.

Croakers are found mostly in bays, inlets, tidal rivers, and along the surf. They like shallow water over grassy or sandy flats. You can catch croakers in the daytime, but some of the best fishing takes place at night. Croakers are caught all year round in southern waters and from June to October in northern waters.

Since it is a small fish it should be caught on light tackle for the most sport. A spinning outfit is ideal for them. Use small No. 1 or 1/0 hooks baited with sea worms, pieces of clam, squid, shedder crab, or shrimp.

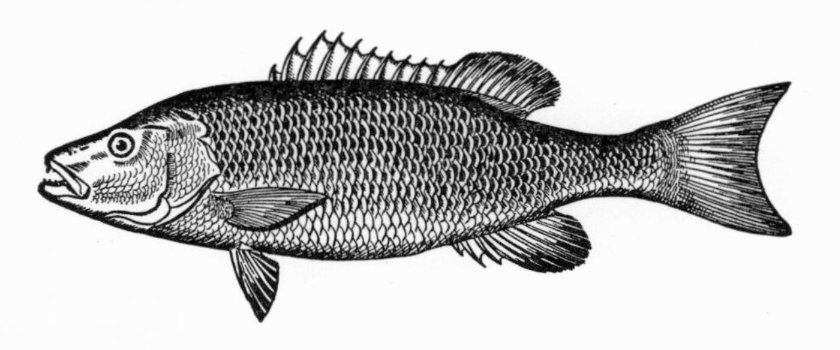

MANGROVE SNAPPER

SNAPPERS

In tropical waters one of the largest families of bottom fish are the snappers. At least 250 species are found in the warm waters of the world. Some snappers, such as the red snapper, grow big, often reaching a weight of 35 pounds. Red snappers are most plentiful in deeper offshore waters on so-called "snapper banks." Red snappers are caught only with strong tackle. Use 5/0 or 6/0 hooks baited with small fish or chunks of mullet.

Another snapper which is often caught is the mangrove snapper. It gets its name because it is often found around mangrove-tree roots. Mangrove snappers are also found around jetties, piers, bridges, and coral reefs. They don't grow as large as the red snapper, so you can use a smaller hook such as the Eagle Claw No. 2/0, 3/0, or 4/0. Mangrove snappers bite on live shrimp, small fish, cut mullet, and crabs. They will also often strike artificial lures and so can be caught quite easily on plugs, spoons, and jigs.

There are many other snappers, such as the lane snapper, dog snapper, schoolmaster, muttonfish, and yellowtail, which can be caught in the same waters. They can be fished for with the same hooks and baits as those used for mangrove snappers.

GROUPERS

Another large group of bottom fishes in tropical waters are the groupers. There are many different kinds, such as the Nassau grouper, black grouper, yellow grouper, rock grouper, and the red grouper.

Groupers are usually found around coral reefs, rocks, sunken wrecks, and piers and bridges. They are strong fish which often succeed in tangling your line in underwater obstructions and cutting it off, so you need a rather stiff rod and strong monofilament line when fishing for them.

Most of the groupers reach a large size and have

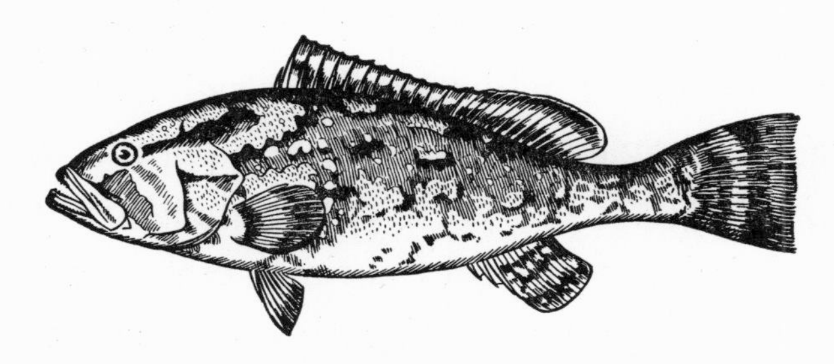

RED GROUPER

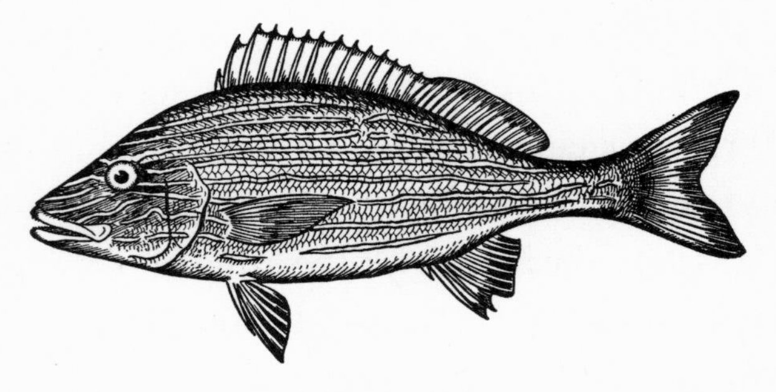

YELLOW GRUNT

big mouths, so hooks running from 4/0 to 8/0 can be used. They will bite on live or dead fish such as whole or chunk mullet, grunts, and sardines. Groupers will also take live or dead shrimp when used as bait.

GRUNTS

The grunts are very numerous in warm seas. They do not grow very big, averaging about 1 pound or less in weight, but they are plentiful, and large catches are often made. Some of the grunts which are caught are the margate, the gray grunt, blue-striped grunt, white grunt, French grunt, black margate, yellow grunt, porkfish, and pigfish.

Small No. 1 or 1/0 hooks are used for grunts, and such baits as pieces of shrimp, crab, sea worm, clams, or fish are used. For the most sport, light tackle should be used, and a spinning outfit is ideal.

OTHER BOTTOM FISH

There are many other bottom fish which can be caught in salt water in the Atlantic and Pacific oceans and the Gulf of Mexico. Such fish as the spot or Lafayette, haddock, pollack, silver hake or whiting, line, and herring are caught in the Atlantic. In tropical waters you can catch jewfish, sheepshead, pompano, angelfish, and catfish. In Pacific waters there are halibut, spotfin croakers, yellowfin croakers, corbina, rockfish, surf perch, ling cod, cabezon, and greenlings.

Surf fish

The surf fisherman depends on his own knowledge of the best spots to fish. The easy way to locate the best fishing spot is to ask a friend or a fishing tackle dealer who knows where the fish have been running recently. If the newspaper in your area has an outdoor column you can often read where the fish have been biting recently. Down by the beach you can often locate the best fishing spot by looking for other surf anglers who may be catching fish. If you see several surf anglers lined up in one spot, then it's a good idea to try your luck there, too. If you can't find out where the fish are biting from other anglers you must try to locate them yourself. At the beach look for gulls or terns screaming and diving into the water. These birds feed on the smaller fish which are chased to the surface by the larger fish. Sometimes you can see the smaller fish leaping out of the water, trying to get away from the larger fish, or one of the big fish may come up and splash on top of the water.

If you can't see any birds or fish you must fish in the most likely spots. Usually the best fishing takes place in the deeper holes and channels near shore. You can locate these by looking for blue or dark-green water. Lighter-colored water and white water caused by breaking waves indicate shallower spots. Here you will often find a sand bar, rocky reef, or shallow area. These spots are sometimes good for striped bass when the water is rough.

Along sandy beaches one good method of fishing is to walk along the beach and make a cast or two every 50 feet or so with an artificial lure such as a metal squid or plug.

Along rocky shores the best spots to fish are rocky points and coves. Those areas which have sunken or exposed rocks showing are worth trying. Striped bass like to lie near such rocks, especially when the water is rough.

If there are any jetties or breakwaters, you can

try casting from these. Usually the best spot on a jetty is near the front, where you can cast into deep water. But fish such as striped bass and bluefish are also caught in the shallower water near shore and alongside the rocks of the jetty or breakwater.

If there is an inlet or river emptying into the ocean this is one of the best spots to fish. Here you will find many surf fish waiting for the smaller bait fish which enter and leave such inlets or rivers. Usually the best time to fish such locations is when the tide is going out.

Just as important as picking the best spot is choosing the best time to go surf fishing. You'll catch more fish if you go out early in the morning, just as the sun is rising. Another good time to fish is in the evening, when the sun is setting. Many surf anglers also fish at night. This can be a lot of fun when the moon is shining, but fish are also caught on the darkest nights. You need a good headlight or searchlight when fishing at night.

Striped bass are easier to catch when the water is rough than when it is calm and clear. When big waves are rolling in and breaking on shore you will often find striped bass feeding in the white water. Good surf fishing is often found right after a storm. However, if the water gets too brown or too dirty with seaweed or debris, the fishing is usually poor. Then you must wait until the water gets clean again.

A good surf fisherman also knows how to use his lures or baits to get the most bites or strikes. When surf fishing, you have to watch the waves closely. Wait till a big wave approaches and then cast behind or beyond the wave. As you reel the lure in, vary the speed. Turn the reel handle fast when a wave carries the lure toward you. Turn it slower when the current or backwash pulls the lure away from you.

For bluefish and small striped bass you should reel a metal squid faster than for big striped bass or weakfish. Try to imitate a wounded bait fish with your lure. Surface plugs should be worked fairly fast and jerked at regular intervals to create a splash on top of the water. Underwater plugs should be reeled in at a medium or slow speed. All lures should be reeled more slowly at night than in the daytime. And when the water is calm and clear, fast reeling often produces better results than slow reeling. At all times it pays to change lures until you find one which the fish like.

When the fish refuse to take artificial lures in the surf, you can often catch them on natural baits. You can bait your hook with a piece of mullet or menhaden, sea worm, crab, squid, or shrimp, and cast out as far as you can. Then reel in slowly, letting the bait stay a minute or two in a new spot each time. Keep doing this until the bait is near the beach. Then reel in and cast out again. When you feel a bite, let the fish swallow the bait. When the fish starts to move off, strike hard to set the hook.

The kind of fish you will catch from the surf depends on where you live and fish. The following are the most common and popular surf fish.

STRIPED BASS

The striped bass is caught in the surf from Virginia to Maine along the Atlantic Coast and around San Francisco along the Pacific Coast. A striped bass is easily recognized by the 7 or 8 stripes on its sides. It has an olive-green back and silvery sides. Most of the striped bass you catch will run anywhere from 1 to 20 pounds in weight. But many fish weighing 30, 40, and 50 pounds are caught.

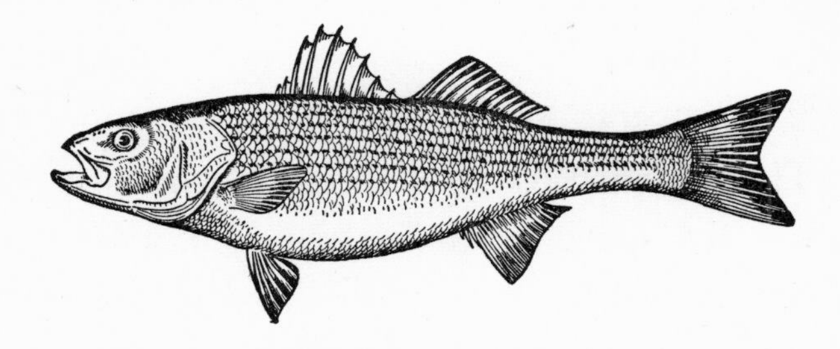

STRIPED BASS

You can catch striped bass in the surf on a wide variety of lures and baits. They take metal squids, plugs, spoons, jigs, rigged eels, and eelskin lures. They bite on such natural baits as bloodworms, sandworms, shedder crabs, shrimp, clams, squid, and small fish such as mullet, menhaden, and butterfish. For small striped bass, No. 4/0, 5/0, or 6/0 hooks should be used; for large striped bass, No. 7/0, 8/0, and 9/0 hooks are used. The Eagle Claw and O'Shaughnessy patterns are good hooks for bass.

In the surf look for striped bass around rock and wood jetties, breakwaters, and piers. They are often found along rocky shores and sandy beaches. Early in the morning, at dusk, and throughout the night are the best times to catch striped bass. They like rough water and are often caught during and after a storm.

The best striped-bass fishing along the Atlantic Coast takes place in the spring and fall. June, September, October, and November are good months.

BLUEFISH

The bluefish is another fish which is often caught in the surf along the Atlantic Coast from Cape Cod to Florida. It gets its name from the blue-green color of its back. The bluefish has a large mouth

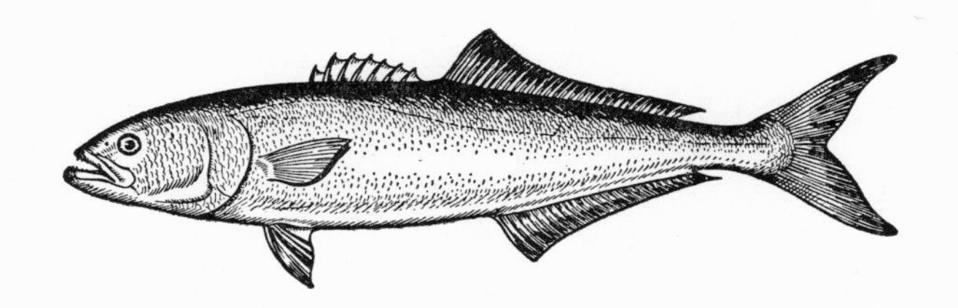

BLUEFISH

armed with many sharp teeth. Most of the bluefish caught in the surf will run from 2 to 6 pounds. However, there are times when larger blues weighing from 8 to 14 pounds appear near the beaches.

Bluefish are unpredictable fish and it is difficult to tell when and where they may appear. Some years they disappear entirely along the Atlantic. When they are present, they are usually caught in the surf from June to October in northern waters and during the winter months in Florida. You can usually locate bluefish, and, of course, other game fish as well, by watching for gulls or terns wheeling and diving excitedly near the beach or shore.

You can catch bluefish on such lures as metal squids, jigs, or plugs. They also take rigged eels and eelskin lures. They bite on natural baits such as small fish or pieces of fish cut from menhaden, mullet, or butterfish. The hooks should be between No. 5/0 and No. 8/0, depending on the size of the fish. The Eagle Claw is a favorite pattern. The hooks should be attached to a cable or single-strand wire leader, since a bluefish's teeth can bite through ordinary line or leader.

Bluefish usually like a fast-moving lure, so when you see them feeding, cast a metal squid out and reel it in as fast as you can turn the handle.

CHANNEL BASS

The channel bass is a favorite fish with surf anglers from Virginia to the Gulf of Mexico. It is most plentiful along the beaches of North Carolina, where it is caught from April to November.

Channel bass are large, copper-colored fish with big mouths and heads. At the base of the tail there is a black spot. Channel bass usually run from 10 to 30 pounds in the surf but big fish up to 50 and even 60 pounds are sometimes caught.

You can catch channel bass with the same surf-fishing rods and reels used for striped bass. They also

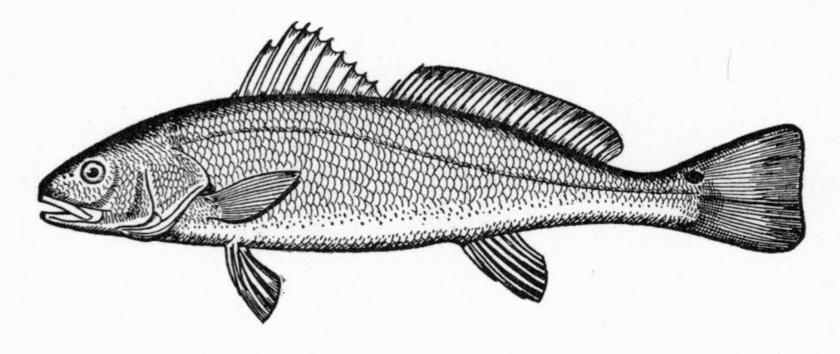

CHANNEL BASS

take the same lures: metal squids, spoons, and plugs. But most surf fishing for channel bass is done with natural baits such as pieces of mullet, menhaden, squid, shrimp, or crab. For small channel bass you can use hooks No. 5/0 or 6/0. For big fish, hooks in sizes 7/0, 8/0, and 9/0 are used.

When found in the surf, the channel bass prefer the bars, holes, and channels. Sometimes they can be seen chasing menhaden or other small fish, but most of the time you have to cast out to a likely spot and let the bait lie there. Give the channel bass plenty of time to take the bait before trying to set the hook.

The best months for channel-bass fishing along the Atlantic Coast are April, May, October, and November. In Florida the winter months are often good. Fish for channel bass early in the morning and in the evening for best results.

WEAKFISH

There are two kinds of weakfish caught by surf anglers along the Atlantic Coast. One is the common, or northern, weakfish, which is found from Cape Cod to Florida. The other is the spotted, or southern, weakfish, which is often called the sea trout in southern waters. The southern weakfish is found from Virginia to the Gulf of Mexico. The two kinds

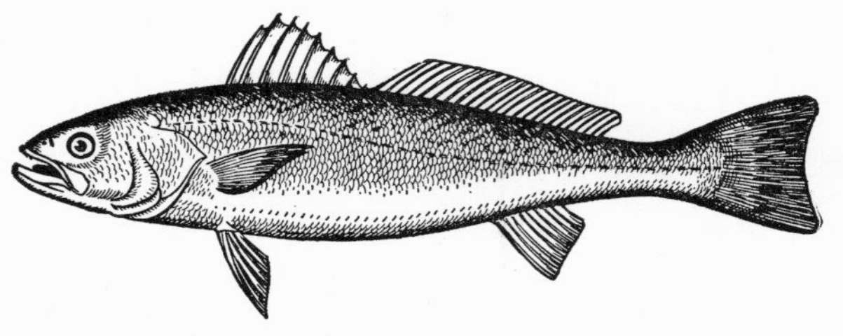

COMMON WEAKFISH

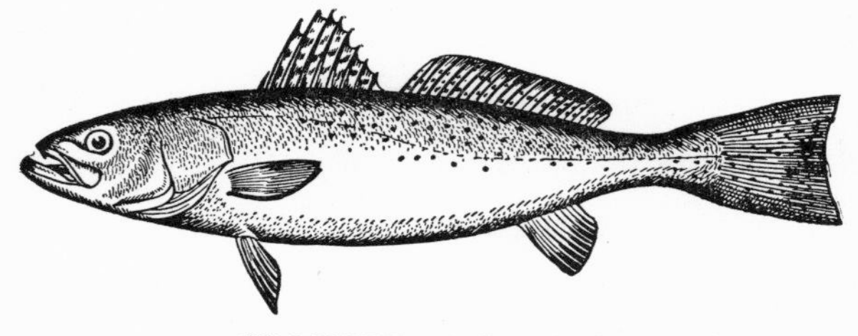

SPOTTED WEAKFISH

TWO KINDS OF WEAKFISH

of weakfish have similar body shapes but the northern weakfish is more colorful, having a variety of colors along its back and sides, with orange or yellow fins. The southern weakfish is mostly silvery, with black spots scattered along the back and sides. Most weakfish will run from 1 to 5 pounds in weight. But occasionally big fish up to 12 pounds may appear in the surf. The northern weakfish grows up to 20 pounds in weight, while the southern weakfish reaches 15 pounds.

Weakfish are caught casting in the surf with such artificial lures as metal squids, jigs, spoons, and small plugs. They are also caught with live baits such as sandworms, squid, shrimp, shedder crab, and pieces of mullet or other small fish. Hooks No. 3/0, 4/0, 5/0, or 6/0 are the best sizes to use.

Weakfish have that name because they have weak mouths which tear easily. Use your lightest tackle for these fish and take care while playing them on the end of a line. Always use a gaff or a net to land a good-sized weakfish. Only the small ones (up to a pound) should be lifted into a boat.

Weakfish can be caught during the day or night. Along the beaches, fish at high tide and in outgoing water. Jetties and breakwaters can be fished at low tide if there is deep water near the end.

WHITING

The whiting is a small fish caught in the surf along the Atlantic Coast and in the Gulf of Mexico.

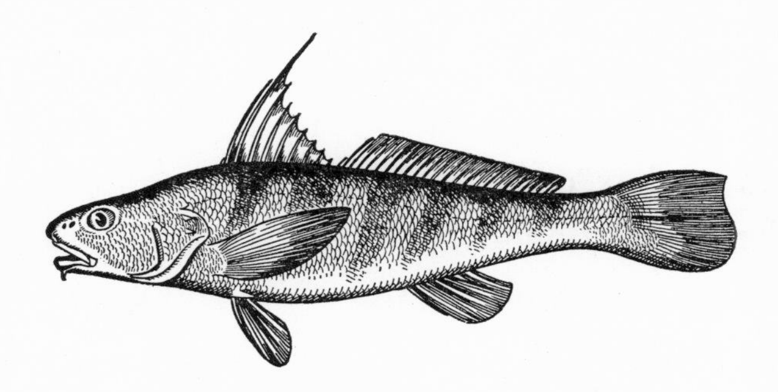

NORTHERN WHITING

Two kinds are usually caught: the northern whiting, found from Massachusetts to Florida and often called the kingfish, and the southern whiting, found from Virginia to Florida. Both types of whiting have small, underslung mouths and vary in color from gray to black, with faint stripes on the sides.

Since whiting average about a pound and rarely reach more than 5 or 6 pounds, light fishing tackle is most suitable for them. A medium-weight surf spinning outfit is ideal. Whiting are caught mostly on live baits such as bloodworms, sand bugs, bits of squid, or pieces of shrimp. These are placed on small hooks such as No. 1/0 Eagle Claw.

Whiting give a very rapid, sharp bite, which you feel as a series of sharp tugs. You should strike back immediately to set the hook: if you wait too long your bait will be stolen.

OTHER FISH

There are many other kinds of fish which can be caught by surf fishing. In northern Atlantic waters anglers catch blackfish, or tautog, pollack, croakers, and flounders. In waters around Florida they catch pompano, jack crevalle, snook, snappers, grunts, and grouper. In California they catch corbina, croakers, rockfish, surf perch, and sharks.

Game fish

The following are the most important game fish caught in offshore waters.

SWORDFISH

The swordfish is an offshore fish which most big-game anglers would like to catch. However, these deep-sea fighters are not plentiful and they are hard to hook. Even after you do hook a swordfish you stand a good chance of losing him when he breaks the line or the hook pulls out of his mouth. Many anglers have fought a swordfish for several hours, only to lose him in the end.

The swordfish is easily recognized by its broad bill, tall dorsal fin, and wide tail. The average swordfish caught on rod and reel will run from 200 to 400 pounds. But in some spots, such as the Pacific Ocean off South America, swordfish weighing anywhere from 500 to 1,000 pounds are caught.

Swordfish are found in many parts of the world,

SWORDFISH

including both the Atlantic and Pacific coasts of the United States. The best fishing days have little wind and calm water. At such times you can often spot swordfish fins above the water. Then the captain of the boat trolls a whole squid or fairly large fish, such as a mackerel, in front of the fish as bait. Mostly swordfish refuse to take the bait, but every so often one will hit it and swallow it, and then the fight begins. If you are lucky and the fish is hooked securely, you may land your swordfish in two or three hours. But if the fish is not hooked properly or is very big, you may have to fight most of the day.

MARLIN

Marlin are also big-game fish which are caught offshore. There are three kinds of marlin caught in the United States: the white marlin, which is the smallest; the striped marlin, which is larger; and the blue marlin, which is the biggest. They all have spears or bills and broad tails. The white marlin and

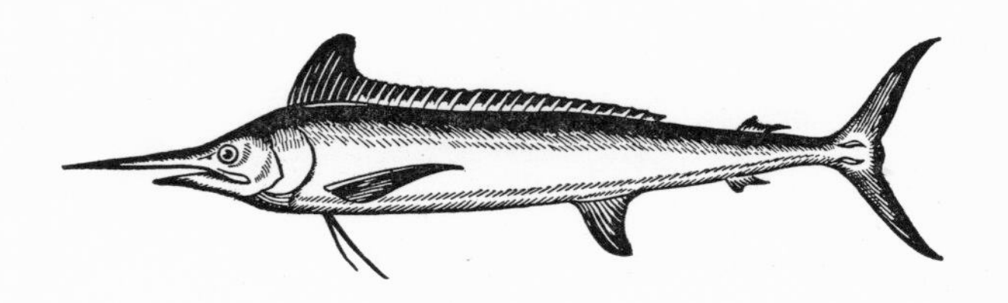

WHITE MARLIN

blue marlin are found along the Atlantic Coast, while the striped marlin is found in Pacific waters.

Marlin are caught by trolling lures or baits well offshore. They will sometimes strike such lures as feather jigs and large plugs, but most of them are caught on dolphin or on whole fish such as mullet, bonito, or mackerel. These are rigged with one or two hooks. Strips cut from these fish are also used.

Marlin usually hit such baits with their bills first; then they return and take the bait into their mouths. That is why outriggers are useful when fishing for marlin. The slack line allows the fish time to swallow the bait. Then, when the line tightens, the rod is brought back hard to set the hook.

Marlin often jump out of the water or "tail-walk" along the surface when hooked. They fight long and hard, and it may take up to two or three hours to land a big fish. However, most white marlin rarely go over 100 pounds, and such a fish can usually be landed in less than an hour. Striped marlin and blue marlin may run several hundred pounds in weight and take more time to land.

SAILFISH

The sailfish looks somewhat like a marlin, but has a slimmer body and a large, fan-like dorsal fin

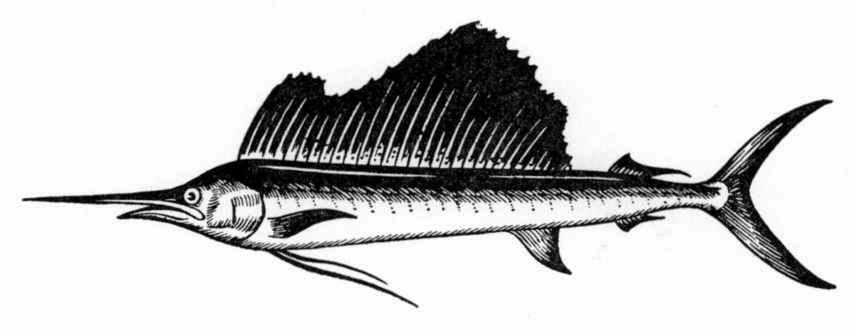

SAILFISH

which gives it its name. There are two kinds of sailfish, the Atlantic sailfish, found mostly off Florida, and the Pacific sailfish, found off Mexico and Lower California.

The Atlantic sailfish rarely reaches more than 100 pounds, but the Pacific sailfish often grows considerably larger.

Sailfish are caught trolling in the same way as marlin, with whole small mullet, or balao, or with fish strips. Sailfish are more plentiful than marlin or other big game fish found in offshore waters. You can charter a boat off Florida for a half day or full day and stand a good chance of hooking one. When a sailfish is hooked he leaps out of the water many times before being boated. Since sailfish are becoming rare and are so large as to be difficult to cook, most of them are released again unless the fish is to be mounted.

TUNA

TUNA

The bluefin tuna is a popular fish with offshore anglers, since it reaches a good size and fights very hard on the end of a line. The smaller tuna, under 100 pounds, are called school tuna; the larger tuna, reaching as much as 800 or 900 pounds, are called giant tuna.

Bluefin tuna are found in both the Pacific and Atlantic oceans. Hooking and landing a giant tuna is not easy. These big tuna are found in only a few spots, and they do not always take a bait. The smaller school tuna, however, are easier to fool and more plentiful. The larger tuna are caught on whole fish such as herring, mackerel, whiting, or menhaden. The school tuna are caught trolling with feather jigs, metal squids, spoons, or plugs.

When a good-sized tuna is hooked it takes off many yards of line at a fast speed, not only once but many times. A school tuna under 100 pounds can be landed in an hour or less; a giant tuna may fight for several hours.

OTHER FISH

Many other fish, such as dolphin, albacore, and bonito, are caught in offshore waters. In southern waters one can also catch barracuda, king mackerel, wahoo, amberjack, and sharks.

Offshore fishing also offers the possibility of seeing such big sea creatures as turtles, porpoises, or, perhaps, if you're lucky, a whale.

17 · Care and Repair of Fishing Tackle

Fishing tackle can be expensive if you have to buy a new rod, reel, line, or lure very often. However, by taking proper care of your fishing tackle, you can make it last a long time. You can also save money by repairing your own rods, reels, and lures.

The fiber-glass fishing rods used today require little care in order to remain in good condition. After each fishing trip, especially in salt water, the entire fishing rod should be wiped with a rag soaked in fresh water, and then dried with a dry rag. The metal parts, such as the guides, ferrules, and reel seats, should then be wiped with an oily rag. If you do this regularly you will find that the metal parts on the fishing rod will not corrode.

At the beginning of each fishing season the fishing rod should be examined carefully. The heat and dryness of steam-heated rooms and apartments will often loosen the ferrules, reel seat, or top guide on a fishing rod. These can be made tight by heating the metal parts over a gas stove or alcohol lamp. First you should remove the ferrule or reel seat from the rod and heat it over a flame until it is very hot. You can use pliers or gloves to hold the metal part so you won't burn your hands. Then take a stick of ferrule cement and heat it over the flame until it melts. (You can buy this ferrule cement in any fishing tackle store.) Now spread the cement over the part of the fishing rod where the metal part fitted originally. Do this while holding the rod high over the flame so that the cement remains in a liquid state. Then force the ferrule or reel seat back into place. If it doesn't go on easily, hold it over the flame and then push it on.

If there is a lot of space between the reel seat or ferrule and the wooden part of the rod where it fits you may have to add a filler. The best material for this is a few strands of a thread such as bread cord fitted over the wood as shown in the illustration. Then smear on the ferrule cement as before, and force the ferrule or reel seat into place.

If any of the guides on your rod are loose they

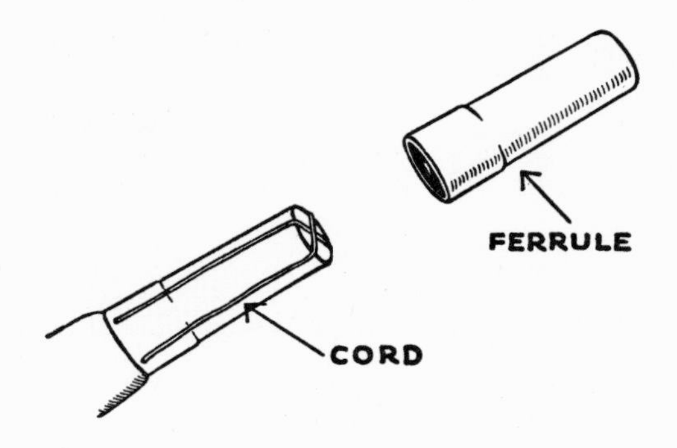

CORD ON ROD TO INSURE
TIGHT FIT OF FERRULE

should be removed, or if the windings holding the guides are old and worn you can remove them all. This is done by cutting the old windings or wrappings with a razor blade or sharp knife. Then you can peel them off and remove the guides. The next step is to take off the old varnish by rubbing the rod with fine steel wool.

The rod is now ready for winding, for which you can use nylon rod-winding thread, which comes in different sizes and colors. For light, thin, fresh-water fishing rods a size No. A winding thread is best. For the heavier, thicker, salt-water rods a No. D winding thread is better. The only real trick to winding a rod is to start and finish properly. To start the winding, tuck the end of the thread under the first few turns until it is buried (see *A* in next drawing).

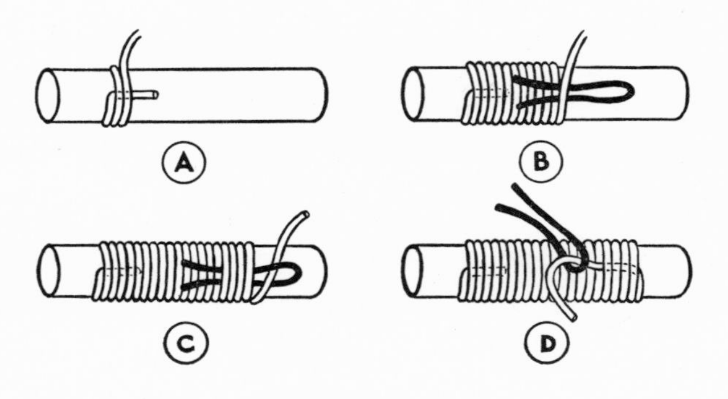

WINDING A ROD

Then continue wrapping until you are ready to finish. Stop a few turns from the end and take a short piece of thread, form a loop, and place it over the end of the winding. The loop should face out past the last winding on the rod. (See *B*.) Now make several more turns of thread over the loop. Then take the end of the winding and run it through the eye of the loop (*C*). Now take the two ends of the buried loop and pull the end of the winding under the last turns. This buries the end of the thread under the winding (*D*).

After the winding is completed, take a comb or a round piece of smooth plastic or celluloid and rub the windings to flatten the thread and close up any spaces between the strands. Now get some color preservative and apply it over the nylon windings. You can buy a small bottle of this color preservative in any fishing tackle store. Two or three coats should be applied, allowing each to dry first. This is done to preserve the true colors of the thread when the rod is varnished.

Now the rod is ready for its first coat of varnish. For best results use a soft, flat brush to apply the varnish. You'll also get a smoother job if you varnish the rod in a warm room free from dust. After you varnish the rod hang it up to dry. A day or two later rub down the first coat of varnish with fine steel wool lightly. Then you can apply the second coat of varnish. When this dries, rub it down with steel wool again. Do this after each coat until four or five coats of varnish have been applied.

Fishing reels also require some care if you want to avoid trouble later. After each fishing trip it's a good idea to wipe the reel with a damp rag. This is especially important with salt-water reels. Some anglers even thoroughly wash their reels in fresh water. Then the reel should be wiped until it is completely dry. After the reel is dry it can be wiped with an oil-soaked rag. Then oil and grease the moving parts of the reel before putting it away. Reels should also be oiled and greased before each fishing trip.

Once or twice a year you can give your reel a thorough cleaning by washing it in kerosene. To do this use a stiff brush to get into the corners and tight spots. First, however, you should take the reel apart so that the gears and working parts are exposed. Then wipe the reel dry, and oil and grease the moving parts thoroughly.

If your fishing reel is not working properly or requires a major overhaul, it should be sent to the factory for a complete checkup and repairs. The best time to do this is during the winter months, when you don't need the reel and the factory has plenty of time to do a good job.

Fishing lines require less care than rods and reels, since nowadays most of them are made from synthetic materials which do not rot. However, fly-casting lines do require some care, especially during the winter months. Do not leave the fly line on the fishing reel, but coil it loosely in a large cardboard box or wind it around a large cylindrical object. Before you do this wash the line in clean fresh water, then dress it with the special fly dressing sold in most fishing tackle stores.

Other fishing lines, such as braided lines and monofilament lines, can be left on the reel, but even here it is a good idea to wash the line first with clean fresh water, especially if it has been used in salt water. It is also a good idea to examine the first few feet of any line to see if it is badly worn or frayed. If it looks weak, cut off the bad section. If the line on your reel is too short to fill the reel spool properly, you can put old fishing line under the good line as backing.

Fishing lures require a great deal of care and repair, especially if they are used in salt water. The hooks and other metal parts rust or corrode. Paint on wooden plugs tends to chip or crack. The finishes on spoons and spinners corrode or tarnish.

If a wooden plug is slightly chipped or cracked it can be touched up with enamel paint or lacquer and a small brush; but if it is badly cracked or chipped it must be repainted completely. First, sandpaper the plug to remove some of the old paint and make it rough. Then paint the plug with white enamel or lacquer. It may need two or three coats of white paint to cover the old paint and wood thoroughly. After the white paint is dry you can add other colors in combination. Of course, if you have an artist's air-brush, you can spray colors galore on the plugs.

Spoons and spinners if tarnished or corroded can be made bright by washing them in soap and lukewarm water and then polishing them with a metal polish and a cloth.

If the feathers or bucktail wound around any of

the hooks of jigs and metal squids are badly worn they can be cut off with a razor blade or knife. Then tie new feathers or bucktail around the hook.

Hooks that are badly rusted should be replaced with new ones. Make sure you get the same size. If the hooks are only slightly rusty they can be cleaned with steel wool and emery cloth and then wiped with an oily rag. Paint the hooks to keep them from rusting too quickly.

Check also the points and barbs on all your hooks. Make sure the points are sharp and not bent or broken. If any hooks are dull they should be sharpened with a small file or sharpening stone.

Taking care of your fishing tackle may seem like a lot of trouble. But it is important to make sure that your fishing tackle is in good condition at all times. You never know when you will hook a big fish, and if any part of your tackle is weak you may lose him.

18 · Sportsmanship

Fishing is a sport which has very few rules or regulations. Other sports, such as baseball, basketball, tennis, and golf, for example, have to be played under strict official rules. But fishing has no such official rules and you are free to fish in any way you please.

However, there are some unwritten laws which are practiced and observed by most anglers who try to be good sportsmen. The main reason for going fishing is to have fun. At the same time, a good sportsman doesn't interfere with another angler's fishing. Because more and more people are fishing today, the popular spots are usually crowded, especially so on weekends and holidays. But a few rules of behavior will make fishing a pleasure even in crowded spots.

Always remember, for example, that when fishing a trout stream, the angler who arrives first at a certain pool or section of the stream is entitled to fish that spot without being crowded. This is especially true if the pool is small. If an angler can reach almost every section of the pool with a cast, then there is room for only one trout fisherman. If the pool is long or wide, there may be room for more than one. But fishermen should be able to stand at least 100 feet away from each other. In some streams trout fishermen stand shoulder to shoulder, especially when the fishing season has just opened, but expert trout fishermen avoid such spots. There are usually several good pools or fishing areas in a trout stream. If one is taken, walk to the next one.

The same holds true for surf fishing. If an angler is already fishing, stay at least 50 feet or 100 feet away. Even if the surf angler is catching fish it is bad manners to crowd him. A surf angler needs plenty of room to cast in a wide arc and to fight a hooked fish. If you are too close he may lose a hooked fish that has been tangled in your line.

Crowding should also be avoided when you are fishing from a boat. If anglers are anchored over a fishing spot, be sure you are at least 50 feet away from them when you drop your anchor. If they are casting lures, you should stay at least 150 feet from the nearest boat.

Never cut across the lines of a trolling boat. Wait until the boat passes and is at least 200 feet away before cutting in behind it. Otherwise you may entangle his lines in your propeller and cut them off.

If you are fishing from a boat don't come so close to shore that fishermen on the bank can reach you with a cast. You can move all over the lake, river, or ocean but the angler on shore is limited to a few spots. Why spoil his sport and endanger yourself and the occupants of your boat by coming so close that a sinker or hook cast from shore can reach you, possibly injuring someone?

Always be careful of the other fishermen near you, whether you are casting from shore, pier, bridge, or boat. Make sure that no one is behind you when you cast. Always use an overhead cast when casting from a boat or pier. If casting is not allowed on the pier or boat you are fishing from, a sporting fisherman abides by the rules.

When fishing from a crowded pier or party boat, let out your line as straight as possible so it does not tangle with the lines of the other anglers. Many tangles are not caused by fishermen, but by the current, tide, or movement of the boat or a hooked fish. If lines get tangled, try to help straighten them out as soon as possible. And if you tangle with another's line, don't blame him, even if it is his fault. The next time *you* may be to blame.

A good sportsman obeys all the fish laws regarding open seasons, size limits, and bag limits. Don't try to fish without a fishing license in fresh water if you are at the age or in a state which requires such a license. These licenses provide the money used to improve the fishing in a lake or stream. If there were no fishing licenses there would be fewer fish and fewer spots in which to catch them.

If the law says that you should throw back all fish under a certain size, don't try to keep the small fish. If you are allowed to keep only a certain number of bass or trout, don't try to sneak any extra fish home. And if the season is closed on a certain kind of fish, don't try to catch them. If you do catch one by accident, remove the hook carefully and throw the fish back into the water.

Most salt-water fish may be caught in any quantities or size. A few fish, such as the striped bass or snook, may be protected; but others can be taken in large numbers, and some anglers bring them home by the bagful. If the fish are very plentiful, no harm is done. But if the fish are thrown away without being eaten, the waste is unsporting. If you take too many fish or keep too many small ones, then you are reducing the number of fish which can be caught in the coming years. Most anglers would rather catch one big fish than several smaller ones. So throw back the small fish, and give them a chance to grow up into worth-while trophies.

Fishing clubs are usually the centers of good sportsmanship. If you enjoy fishing you will probably enjoy the friendliness of a club. You will meet other anglers, some of whom are experts. They are always glad to advise beginners. Many clubs hold casting classes and fishing contests to improve your skill. They have instruction classes for making lures and other tackle. They provide pleasant companions to take along on a fishing trip. Joining a fishing club is usually the quickest and happiest way to become a good angler.

Good fishing to you!

Index

About the Author

VLAD EVANOFF is vitally interested in all types of outdoor sports, but fishing is his favorite. His travels to many parts of the United States were planned as fishing trips. He particularly enjoys making his own equipment, and he included such information in *A Complete Guide to Fishing* so that others might share this more unusual aspect of fishing. Mr. Evanoff learned to fish when he was a young boy, but he learned by trial and error and would have welcomed a book such as he has now written.

Mr. Evanoff originally studied at Cooper Union to be a commercial artist, but he changed his plans after the war. Now writing is his major concern, although he frequently illustrates his work. He has contributed numerous articles to the top outdoor sports magazines and fishing guides and is the author of *Surf Fishing, Natural Baits for Fishermen, Spin Fishing,* and *How to Make Fishing Lures.*